BOOKWORMS & JELLYBELLIES

RANJINI RAO & RUCHIRA RAMANUJAM

hachette
INDIA

Ranjini Rao and **Ruchira Ramanujam** are two best friends, whose brainchild, Tadka Pasta, isn't just a food blog they started in 2011, when in the US. It is a repertoire of stories and recipes from their own kitchens – where they learnt to rise above burnt breads and picky-eating phases of their girls – and from the tastes and traditions they've picked up during their travels.

With two books published in quick succession: *Mango Masala – 60 Indian Recipes from Your Local Supermarket* (eBooks2go) and *Around the World with the Tadka Girls* (Westland-Tranquebar), they began to see food literature in a new light.

Upon returning to India a few years ago, they took their love for food, books and children forward through many avenues, right from conducting workshops for children in schools and summer camps – with a focus on the nutritional and cultural aspects of food – to designing healthy and fun recipes for children's menus for clients. They won the FICCI FLO Bangalore Women of the Year Award in 2016, for their work in the local food and culture scene.

They live in Bengaluru, where they often discuss plots and plans over endless cups of filter coffee. They love chillies, chocolate and everything in between, and can twist themselves up into pretzels for a plate of good food.

We dedicate this book to our marshmallow tootsies – our daughters, who are also best friends, like us, and our biggest fans.

First published in 2017 by Hachette India
(Registered name: Hachette Book Publishing India Pvt. Ltd)
An Hachette UK company
www.hachetteindia.com
This black-and-white edition published in 2026

SRD

Paperback ISBN 978-93-5731-844-0

Hachette Book Publishing India Pvt. Ltd
4th & 5th Floors, Corporate Centre,
Plot No. 94, Sector 44, Gurugram - 122003, India

Typeset in ABeeZee 9/9.5
by Manmohan Kumar, New Delhi

Printed and bound in India by
Manipal Technologies Limited, Manipal

INTRODUCTION

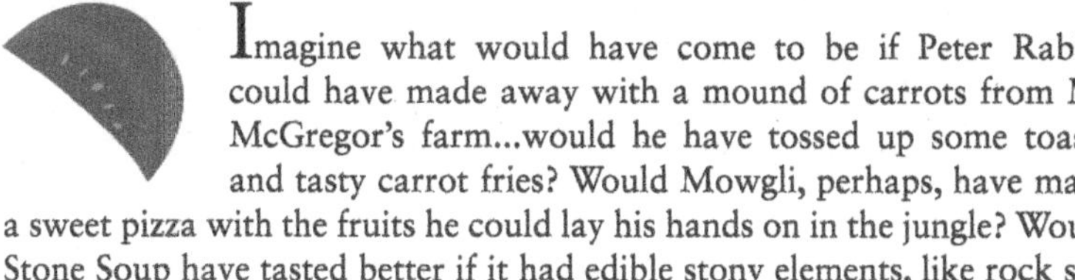

Imagine what would have come to be if Peter Rabbit could have made away with a mound of carrots from Mr McGregor's farm...would he have tossed up some toasty and tasty carrot fries? Would Mowgli, perhaps, have made a sweet pizza with the fruits he could lay his hands on in the jungle? Would Stone Soup have tasted better if it had edible stony elements, like rock salt and lumpy jaggery?

There are so many children's books that fill us with a craving for food, either by design or otherwise. Growing up as avid readers ourselves, we have often spent dreamy afternoons putting together backyard parties for our friends, inspired by the mad tea party in *Alice in Wonderland*. We would assemble little cupcakes with blobs of jam on a tray, labelled 'Eat me!' and bring out a pitcher filled with lemonade, labelled 'Magic Potion.' We would stare long and hard at little nooks in our gardens hoping they would magically turn into secret passageways, just like in Alice's Wonderland.

And now, our daughters, who are always hungry for 'something special,' especially if the hint comes from a book, have given us enough food for thought on these lines. With mouthwatering descriptions tucked between paragraphs in favourite books that have been read over and over again, and recipe ideas that seem to just roll out of certain characters' mouths, we seem to have gathered a long list of bookish recipe ideas.

We have also stood on the sidelines and marvelled at the creative skills of our girls in putting little treats together, mostly as a happy conclusion to even the grimmest of storylines. Whether it is the gummy layers of jam sandwiched between slices of bread for breakfast, lunch and dinner, in the excitement of being very much like Frances in *Bread and Jam for Frances*, or honey drizzled over pancakes and just about everything, given that it was Winnie-the-Pooh's absolute favourite, we've seen it all.

This project is a delightful result of all these experiences, and we hope the readers – the tiny tots as well as the teens – will enjoy this merry ride into the world of books and food. We also hope that this book will excite them enough to scramble to the kitchen and rustle up the listed treats. Above all that, we sincerely hope that our endeavour will inspire children to read more and appreciate the food that gets to the table every day.

It's unfortunate that some popular and highly inspirational books (like Harry Potter) couldn't be included in this repertoire, owing to legal constraints, even though we had worked out the thematic layouts and recipes for them.

Ranjini and Ruchira

FOREWORD

What makes a good children's story? A tight plot, lots of action, sparkling dialogue, strong characters, a decent number of laughs, a hopeful ending? Sure. But what makes a GREAT children's story? In my humble (and hungry!) opinion, the best kind of children's story is one that has a tonne of scrumdiddlyumptious food in it!

If you think that is somewhat shallow of me, I have a good excuse – my childhood. You see, I grew up on a steady diet of Enid Blyton books, and the children in them were constantly eating. They were either picnicking in a field, with jugs of creamy milk and hard-boiled eggs and ham and tongue sandwiches and thick slices of Joanna the cook's fruit cake, or treating themselves to scones with strawberry jam and fresh cream at little village teashops or breaking out tins of fudge, sardines and potted meat, bottles of ginger beer, cream buns, and of course, birthday cake, at midnight feasts. When I took a break from Blyton to read Archie comics, which all circulating libraries of my day were packed to the rafters with, there was no way to escape Pop Tate's soda fountain and All-American burgers. Seriously, what's a (South Indian vegetarian) girl to do when faced with such a cornucopia of delights but to sigh contentedly, surrender and vote with her feet for these stories?

So when I grew up and started writing myself, I simply put food into all my stories. Whether the story was around math, friendship or personal space, whether it was a fantasy story, or a sci-fi one, or historical fiction, there was always food in it. When the action happened in an entirely different universe, as it did in my series Taranauts, I simply made up dishes that I thought children of that universe would like and put those in!

Never in my wildest dreams did I imagine that someone would enjoy reading about my fantasy food so much that they would actually create a recipe for one of those dishes – and put it in a book! But that's exactly what Ranjini and Ruchira have done in *Bookworms & Jellybellies*. What's more, they've created several other recipes for yummylicious food that pair perfectly with other fabulous children's books too! Snacks to crunch on while devouring one book, things to munch on while falling through the rabbit hole of another, drinks to slurp up while chortling (and then – cough, cough – choking!) at the shenanigans of yet another...

What an absolutely terrific idea, right? And just how creative are these two chefoodies (you know, chef + foodies!). The best part? There is so much Indian 'book chow' in there as well.

But we must not be shallow. And this book is anything but. As you drool your way through it, you will not only be introduced to exciting new recipes, but also to so many exciting books that you may never have heard of. In short, it is a feast for both the mind and the palate. Or, in other words, a feast for both the bookworm and the jellybelly.

Bon appétit!

Roopa Pai
August 2017

Roopa Pai is one of India's best-known children's writers. Her books include India's first fantasy-adventure series Taranauts, the award-winning best-seller *The Gita for Children* and *Ready! 99 Must-have Skills for the World-Conquering Teenager (and Almost-Teenager).*

CONTENTS

SECTION TWO (6-9 YEARS)

SECTION THREE (10–14 YEARS)

HIGHLIGHTS

- The recipes in this book are categorized based on age and skill level. The recipes in Category 1 are simple, more visual in nature and the references are more literal. This changes as the book progresses into Categories 2 and 3, in which they are more inventive and inferential. They are simple enough for kids to make with minimum supervision and adult contribution.
- Every recipe is inspired by food references in the chosen book, or is reflective of the setting or culture in the story.
- All the recipes are vegetarian, with easily available ingredients, with substitutions mentioned where appropriate. Eggs are used in a handful of recipes, and egg-free substitutions are included where possible.
- There are many baking recipes since this is an emerging area of interest for children.
- There is a clear focus on healthy ingredients. Lots of fruits, vegetables, proteins, dairy products and whole grains are used in creative ways for maximum kid-appeal. The food is attractive and colourful without the use of food colours. Recipes encourage the use of atta and jaggery, avoiding white flour and sugar as far as possible.
- Recipes cover a variety of meals, light snacks, after-school snacks, desserts and grab-and-go bites.
- Recipe instructions are written with children in mind, with time, quantities and equipment needed clearly mentioned at the beginning. Ingredients are mostly measured by volume, except where items come packaged by weight (e.g., paneer). Methods are well detailed in numbered steps, using a task-oriented manner with each line requiring the child to perform one composite task.
- The introductions to the recipes are designed to arouse the child's curiosity and interest in reading the chosen book. They also connect the book with the idea of the recipe. They are written in an age-appropriate manner, and can be read to the child, or by the child, depending on the category.
- Apart from write-ups and recipes, there are notes, fun facts, limericks, reading recommendations, related trivia and suggested activities for each book.

KITCHEN GEAR

Baking Tray

Baking Dish

Oven Mitts

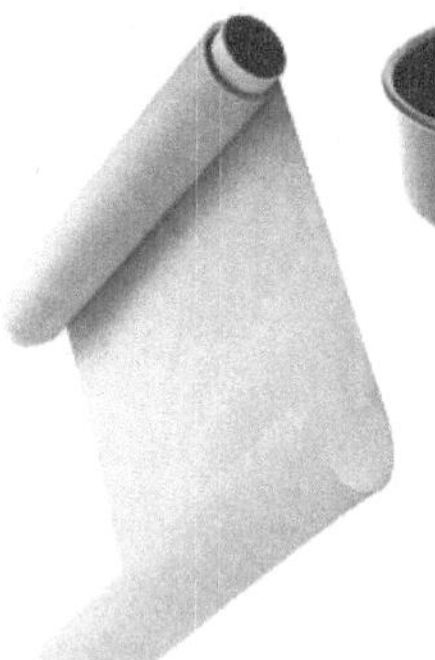
Parchment Paper

Cake Dish

Muffin Cups

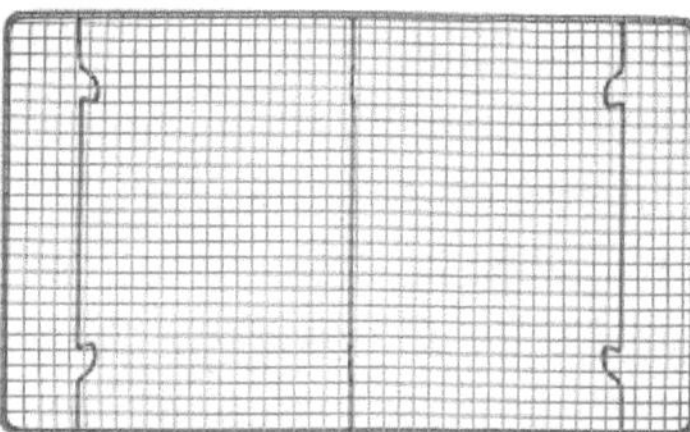
Cooling Rack

Chopping Board

Mixing Bowl

Frying Pan

Tava

Pressure Cooker

Saucepan

Pot with Lid

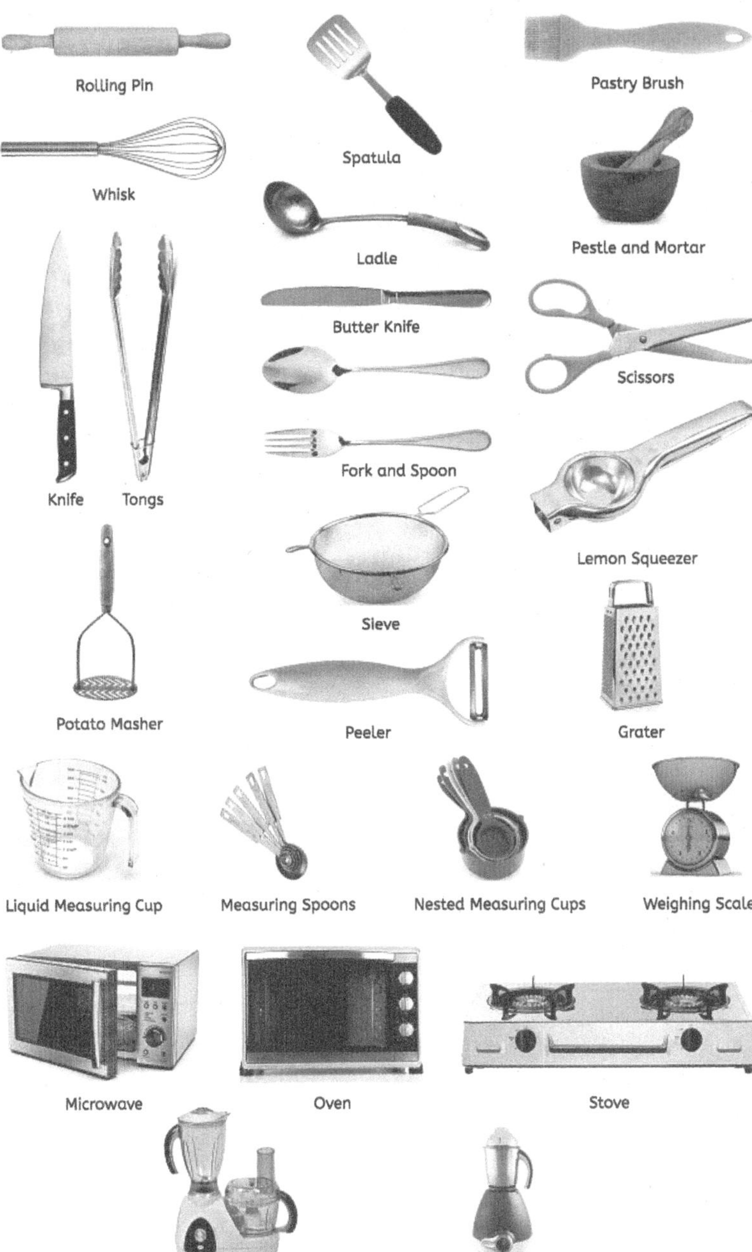
Rolling Pin
Spatula
Pastry Brush
Whisk
Pestle and Mortar
Ladle
Butter Knife
Scissors
Knife
Tongs
Fork and Spoon
Lemon Squeezer
Sieve
Potato Masher
Peeler
Grater
Liquid Measuring Cup
Measuring Spoons
Nested Measuring Cups
Weighing Scale
Microwave
Oven
Stove
Food Processor
Mixer-grinder

INSTRUCTIONS

• Wash and dry your hands before starting to cook. Roll up loose sleeves, tie long hair back and wear an apron.
• Have an adult supervise your work in the kitchen, especially when you are working with heat, sharp tools or electrical equipment.
• Be careful with knives, graters and peelers. Don't wave them in the air, and hold them firmly at a safe distance of at least 2 inches away from the blade, while using. Always place them on the cutting board or counter when you are not using them.
• Keep your ingredients measured and prepped before you start cooking. This all-important step is also known as *mise en place* in French!
• Wash all fruits and vegetables that you're going to cook with, before cutting them. Make sure the chopping board and other tools and equipment are clean, too.
• Work in an orderly manner! Read the recipe before you start, and then reference it once you finish each step. Put away tools and ingredients once you're done using them so that the countertop stays tidy.
• Use oven mitts to handle hot dishes in the oven or microwave. To handle hot things on the stove, use a strong pair of pincers or tongs.
• Don't operate any electrical appliances with wet hands. And make sure water does not come into contact with open sockets, too, to avoid electrical shocks.
• Keep flammable materials like dish towels and paper away from the fire.
• Switch off appliances like the stove and oven once you're done cooking.
• When using the microwave, always use microwave-safe bowls/pans. NEVER use metal or aluminium foil because this can cause an accident.
• Take the time to present your food in an attractive and tasteful manner. Use appropriate dishes to plate your food and consider adding a garnish such as a sprig of fresh herbs.
• Don't forget to wash the used dishes and wipe down the counter once you finish cooking!

SECTION ONE

WINNIE-THE-POOH AND THE HONEY TREE

BY A.A. MILNE

This is the story of Winnie-the-Pooh, the cute and cuddly teddy bear, who has a LARGE appetite and is extremely fond of honey. Pooh wakes up one morning to a honey-less pantry and suddenly sees a bee buzzing by. So, he decides to follow the bee to get some honey right out of its hive, and after a long, adventurous struggle, ends up with a little pain and a lot of pleasure. After getting bitten on his bottom by the queen bee, sadly, he gets stuck in Rabbit's front door. This is thanks to his expanded bottom, which won't come out when he tries to push himself through. But the fun part, of course, is all the honey he gets to eat, from the hive and in Rabbit's house!

This is just a sneak peek into the crazy and goofy adventure of Pooh on the Honey Tree. Do you think we could nudge Pooh into eating a healthy snack with a bit of honey in it rather than a whole pot? Perhaps we could! Let's try these easy and fuss-free, healthy and crunchy bites filled with lots of goodies and see how they work out!

FUN FACT! Did you know that Winnie-the-Pooh was named after a black bear that the author A.A. Milne saw in London Zoo, and a swan he met while on holiday?

HONEY-CRUNCH SNACK BITES

 +  +  + 

⅓ cup peanut butter

3 tbsps honey

½ cup oats

2 tbsps milk powder

 +  + 

2 tbsps chocolate chips

2 tbsps roasted almonds, chopped

2 tbsps dried cranberries, chopped fine

MAKES 10 * PREP TIME: 30 MINS

KITCHEN GEAR: Large bowl, fork, spoon, storage box.

1. In a large bowl, mix together the peanut butter and honey with a fork.

2. Stir the oats and milk powder into the mixture.

3. Now add the chocolate chips, almonds and cranberries, and use clean hands to mix everything together. If the mixture is too dry, add a teaspoon of honey and if you find it too wet, add a teaspoon of oats.

4. Roll the mixture into small balls and place them in a flat box.

5. Store at room temperature for up to 2 days.

TOP TIP! This is a very versatile recipe and you can play around with the ingredients to suit different tastes. Any nuts and dry fruits can be substituted for almonds and cranberries. Skip the chocolate chips and grind up the dried fruit and nuts if you are making this for a young child or like a smoother texture.

To roast almonds, just pop them in the microwave for about a minute, stir them up and repeat for another minute or so.

THE VERY HUNGRY CATERPILLAR
BY ERIC CARLE

A slithery, green, baby caterpillar eats a LOT of food and after resting in its cosy cocoon for a while, turns into something completely different and stunning – a bright and colourful butterfly. The book that tells this story, *The Hungry Caterpillar,* is a very popular one and has sold millions of copies all over the world.

What if we told you that this book is not just about all the food that the hungry caterpillar gobbles up, but also about math (it makes you count the food items), days of the week (the caterpillar was born on a Sunday, and he ate different foods on different days of the week) and science (the stages of a butterfly's life)? Okay, okay, we know we got you at 'makes you count the food items'! Go ahead, count everything that the hungry caterpillar ate, but come back here for some food...er...for thought!

So, do you think eating smaller portions would have helped the caterpillar? Hmm, maybe you could think of the answer while you munch on this fresh and crisp cucumber caterpillar!

RIDDLE ME THIS! If today is Sunday's yesterday, what would tomorrow be?

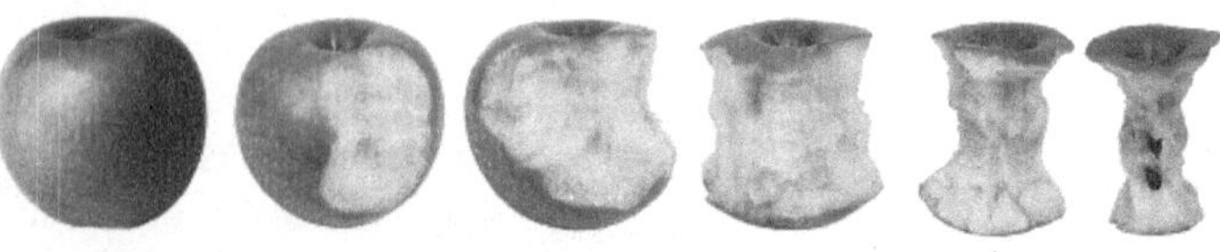

CATERPILLAR CRUNCH SALAD

 +  +  +  +  +

1 medium English cucumber, cut into round slices	1 slice tomato	10–12 sunflower seeds	2 *chironji* seeds	1 almond cut into slivers	Salt and pepper to taste

Salad Dressing

2 tsps strawberry jam + 2 tsps lemon juice + 1 tsp extra virgin olive oil + Salt and pepper to taste

Optional

 + 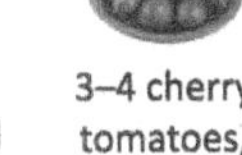 +  +  +  + 

1 lettuce leaf, sliced	3–4 cherry tomatoes, halved	1 baby corn	1 spring onion	1 small carrot, cut into a round slice and a few juliennes	½ cup popcorn

SERVES 1 ✶ PREP TIME: 15 MINS

KITCHEN GEAR: Chopping board, knife, peeler, serving plate.

1. On a plate, arrange the cucumber slices in a curve – like the shape of the caterpillar's body.
2. Place the tomato slice as the cucumber caterpillar's head.
3. Arrange the sunflower seeds below the body as the caterpillar's feet.
4. Place the *chironji* seeds as the caterpillar's eyes.
5. Put a tiny shard of almond as its mouth.
6. Finish by placing two almond slivers on top of its head as the antennae.
7. To make the salad dressing: Put all the ingredients for the dressing in a bottle with a tight-fitting lid. Close the bottle and shake it as hard as you can! Pour the dressing all over the salad, or transfer it to a bowl and just dip and eat.

OPTIONAL: Complete the garden scene with shreds of lettuce as grass. Add cherry tomato halves and baby corn slices as flowers with long spring onion stems. A disc and juliennes of carrot can stand in for the sun and some popcorn can be shaped into puffy clouds.

IF YOU GIVE A MOUSE A COOKIE
BY LAURA JOFFE NUMEROFF

The author of this funny little story says that if you give a mouse a cookie, he'd want a glass of milk to go with it. Do you know anyone else who loves cookies and milk? Wait a minute, do *you* love cookies and milk? What's your favourite cookie to dip into a glass of warm milk?

Anyway, just like the cookie monster in Sesame Street, the mouse in this story doesn't stop at one cookie. The mouse asks for a little bit of this and a little bit of that, and goes all around the house doing all sorts of things... until he's thirsty for some milk... and then... he has to have a cookie with it again.

Phew! Did you find your head going around in circles, just like the mouse in the story? Sit down, please, and have a cookie! Oh, and don't forget the mil... okay, okay, you know what we mean!

RIDDLE ME THIS! What's a dessert with the letters M-O-U-S-E in it?*

*ANS: Mousse, of course!

OATS 'N' CHOCO-CHIP COOKIES

1½ cups oats

+

100g unsalted/cooking butter, soft

+

½ cup brown sugar, firmly packed

+

1 tsp vanilla extract

1 tsp baking soda

+

½ cup chocolate chips

+

1–2 tsps oil for greasing, if using foil

MAKES 15 PREP TIME: 35 MINS BAKING TIME: 15 MINS

KITCHEN GEAR: Mixer-grinder, oven, baking tray, parchment/baking paper or foil, scissors, pastry brush (optional), large microwave-safe bowl, whisk, cling film, cooling rack, oven mitts.

1. Place the butter and brown sugar in a large bowl and whisk well.

2. Stir in the vanilla, powdered oats and baking soda.

3. Mix in the chocolate chips and use your hands to bring the mixture together into a dough.

4. Cover the cookie dough with cling film and refrigerate for about 15 minutes.

5. Meanwhile preheat the oven to 180°C/350°F.

6. Place a piece of parchment paper or aluminium foil on the baking tray. Grease the foil with a little oil, using a pastry brush or your fingers.

7. Take tablespoon-sized lumps of the cookie dough, roll each into a ball and flatten lightly. Put the cookies on the baking tray, about 2 inches apart.

8. Place the tray in the oven and bake for about 15 minutes or until they are slightly browned.

9. Remove the tray from the oven and let the cookies cool on the tray for 5 minutes before moving them to a cooling rack.

10. If you have any more cookie dough leftover, roll and bake the remaining cookies.

11. Let the cookies cool completely and then enjoy them, yes, with a glass of milk.

STONE SOUP
BY MARCIA BROWN

Soups and stories have something in common: they both help us feel a little better, and not just when we are sick. There are many kinds of soups, just as there are stories. How many kinds do you know?

We have all had some variety of soup or the other, but have you ever heard of Stone Soup? Well, the star ingredient, as you can guess from the name is – stone!!

How could a stone possibly make up a delicious soup? It can, as this story tells us, with a little bit of help from other ingredients and seasonings. So, let's take a little help from a grown-up and stir up our own fun version of a Stone-y Soup – which involves some rocks, actually.

What, are you getting set to grind your teeth? Oh, don't worry, they are all edible stones, like 'rock' salt, and 'lumpy' jaggery!

FUN FACT! Did you know that there's a big pool in Oslo, Norway, and it is nicknamed Spikersuppa (Nail Soup)? That is because in Northern Europe, the story is more commonly known as *The Nail Soup!* In fact, Stone Soup is known by many different names around the world, such as button soup, axe soup, wood soup, and so on.

TOMA STONE SOUP

 +  +  +  + 

Stones – 2 small rock salt nuggets or peppercorns	4 ripe tomatoes	2 garlic cloves	1 tbsp tomato paste	½ lump of organic jaggery or 1 tsp sugar

 +  +  +  + 

1 tbsp unsalted/ cooking butter	¼ tsp roasted cumin powder	¼ tsp pepper powder	Salt to taste	A few mint leaves

SERVES 2–3 PREP TIME: 15 MINS COOKING TIME: 15 MINS

KITCHEN GEAR: Pressure cooker, chopping board, knife, ladle, mixer-grinder, soup strainer, pestle and mortar

1. Put the stones (rock salt nuggets or peppercorns) into the pressure cooker.
2. Wash the tomatoes, cut them into quarters and add them to the cooker.
3. Pour 1.5 cups of water into the cooker.
4. Peel the garlic, smash it using a pestle and mortar, and put the pods into the cooker.
5. Add the tomato paste and lump of jaggery to the cooker. Stir well using a ladle.
6. Place the pressure cooker on the stove. Close the lid and bring up to full steam. Once it whistles, reduce the heat to low and cook for about 5 minutes. Switch off the heat and wait until the pressure releases on its own.
7. Once the steam has released, open the cooker and let the soup cool a little.
8. Use a big ladle to smash the tomatoes very well. You can also use a mixer-grinder to do this.

9. Strain the soup into another pot and press the solids to release as much liquid as possible. Discard the strained solids.
10. Add the butter, cumin powder and pepper powder to the soup.
11. Stir well. Taste, and add salt if the soup needs it.
12. If you want, warm the soup before serving.
13. Garnish the soup with mint leaves and add some croutons for crunch.

GOLDILOCKS AND THE THREE BEARS

BY ROBERT SOUTHEY

Have you ever taken a spoonful of ice cream from your sister's bowl when she wasn't looking and licked it clean? Or picked out the pickles from your mom's sandwich when she was too busy serving everyone else? Or maybe you have taken a nap in your dad's bed when he was at work, because his pillow is bigger and fluffier. Didn't every one of those things taste and feel better than your own? Haha, don't worry, we are not going to tell anyone!

This story of Goldilocks tells you why she felt so comfortable in the home of the three bears.

And shhh, don't tell anyone, especially Goldilocks, about the porridge you're going to make and put away in the fridge tonight, for tomorrow's breakfast!

FUN FACT! Did you know that Goldilocks is the nickname of a planet that, like Earth, may possibly have water – and life? It is also the name of a very famous bakery in the Philippines and a flower, too!

OVERNIGHT OATS PORRIDGE

+

+

¼ cup oats

¼ cup milk

2 tsps honey, or to taste

+

½ tsp cocoa powder

1 tbsp creamy peanut butter

SERVES 1 PREP TIME: 10 MINS SOAKING 6–8 HOURS

KITCHEN GEAR: Glass jar with lid, spoon.

1. Add all the ingredients into a glass jar and stir well.

2. Put the jar into the fridge and let it sit overnight or for at least 6 hours.

3. When you are ready to eat, stir the porridge in the jar. You can warm the porridge in the microwave if you don't like to eat it cold.

4. Top the porridge with some fresh fruit and your favourite roasted nuts for a delicious, energy-boosting breakfast right out of a jar.

THE TALE OF PETER RABBIT
BY BEATRIX POTTER

We all know that a rabbit's favourite food is carrot. What's yours? Are you particular about pasta, pizza or pie? Or maybe you're crazy about cookies, canapés and cake? Could it be that you're mad over mangoes, melons or marshmallows?

Whatever your choice may be, if you eat too much of it, it could upset your tummy. And then your mom and dad would probably have to send you to bed with a sip or two of a herbal drink which may not be as yummy as your favourite food after all.

When eating, just like in doing anything else, a little too less isn't quite the best, and a little too much isn't too good, as such. Now, now, if Peter Rabbit hadn't gone on an adventure in Mr McGregor's garden, how would he, or even we, know this?

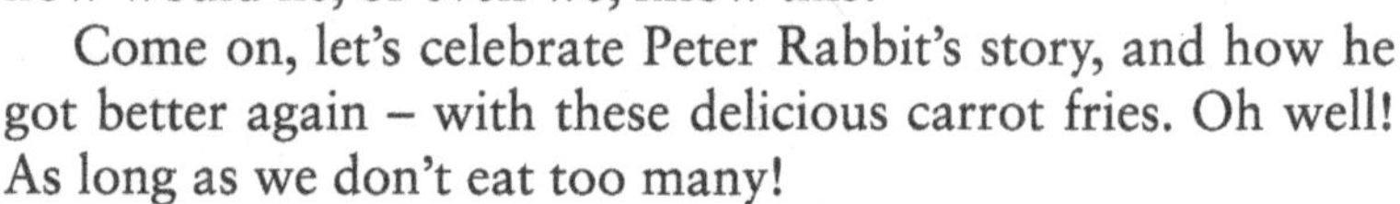

Come on, let's celebrate Peter Rabbit's story, and how he got better again – with these delicious carrot fries. Oh well! As long as we don't eat too many!

FUN FACT! In Japan, the story of Peter Rabbit is really popular, and so are Peter Rabbit toys and mugs, among other things. In fact, there's a theme park and lookalike versions of Potter's house and Mr McGregor's gardens, in Japan!

The delightful treasury of Beatrix Potter's classic stories

PETER RABBIT

THE COMPLETE TALES

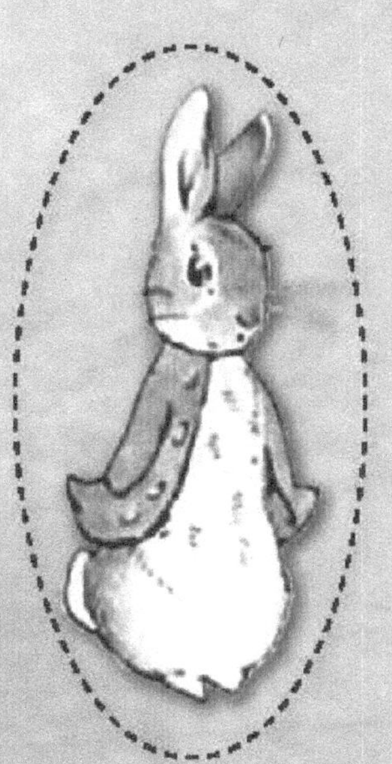

BEATRIX POTTER

SESAME CARROT FRIES

3 large or 6 small carrots

\+ 1 tsp plus 1 tbsp oil

\+ ½ tsp coriander powder

\+ Pinch of red chilli powder (optional)

\+ Pinch of turmeric

\+ Pinch of *garam masala*

\+ Salt to taste

\+ 1 tsp toasted sesame seeds

KITCHEN GEAR: Oven, baking tray, parchment/baking paper or foil, scissors, pastry brush (optional), large mixing bowl, spoon, tongs, serving platter.

1. Preheat the oven to 200°C/ 400°F.

2. Cut a sheet of parchment paper the size of the baking tray. Place it on the tray and set aside. Or use a large piece of aluminium foil to line the tray. Then pour one teaspoon of oil on it and spread it all over, using a pastry brush or your fingers. Set aside.

3. Peel and then cut the carrots into thick sticks shaped like french fries.

4. In a large bowl, pour the tablespoon of oil.

5. Add the coriander powder, chilli powder (if using), turmeric, garam masala, salt and sesame seeds to the oil and stir.

6. Tip in the carrots. Toss well using clean hands.

7. Arrange the carrot sticks in a single layer on the prepared baking tray.

8. Put the tray into the oven and bake for about 30 minutes or until the fries are tender and just start to brown.

9. Remove the tray from the oven and carefully transfer the hot fries to a serving dish using tongs. Serve hot on their own, or with a creamy yogurt dip.

YIPPEE-DIP! To make the yogurt dip, whisk plain yogurt and season it with salt, white pepper, cumin powder, sugar and grated garlic.

GOODNIGHT MOON
BY MARGARET WISE BROWN

Do you have a bedtime routine, say, like listening to a story or a song? Or would you rather just have your mom or dad pat you to sleep while the insects whir softly outside your window? Do you run into everyone's room in the house, hug them tightly and kiss them goodnight, before the lights go out? Have you ever tried drifting to sleep, while counting sheep?

There are so many ways to go to sleep, but the sure winner is when you can say goodnight to everyone and everything, right from your dinner spoon to your favourite cartoon. Or maybe you can listen to the story of *Goodnight Moon*, and go from blink-blink to z-z-z... all too soon!

Before you snooze off and wander into dreamland, how about some mashed potatoes with a big load of cheese? If you'd ask us, we'd say, 'Yes, please!'

TRY THIS! Write down the rhyming words for 'night' and 'moon' and count them. Then, if you're not too tired, try to find words that rhyme with 'orange,' or 'purple,' and let us know if you have any luck with those!

SWEET POTATO MISHMASH

1 medium-sized freshly boiled sweet potato*

+

¼ cup milk

+

1 tbsp salted butter

Salt and pepper to taste

+

A small piece of Cheddar cheese

SERVES 2 (OR 1 VERY HUNGRY PERSON) * PREP TIME: 15 MINS

KITCHEN GEAR: Medium bowl, small microwave-safe bowl, potato masher or fork, serving bowl, spoon.

1. Peel the sweet potato and place it in a medium bowl. Set aside.

2. Put the milk and butter in a small microwave-safe bowl and microwave for about 30 seconds, or until the milk is warm and the butter melts.

3. Pour the milk and butter mixture all over the sweet potatoes.

4. Sprinkle with plenty of salt and pepper.

5. Mash the sweet potato well using a potato masher or fork and then whip it well.

6. Transfer the potato mash to a serving bowl and grate the cheese all over the top.

7. Serve immediately.

*Sweet potatoes can get mushy when overcooked. Do make sure that the sweet potato is firm to the touch, but tender inside.

AN IDENTITY CARD FOR KRISHNA

BY DEVDUTT PATTANAIK

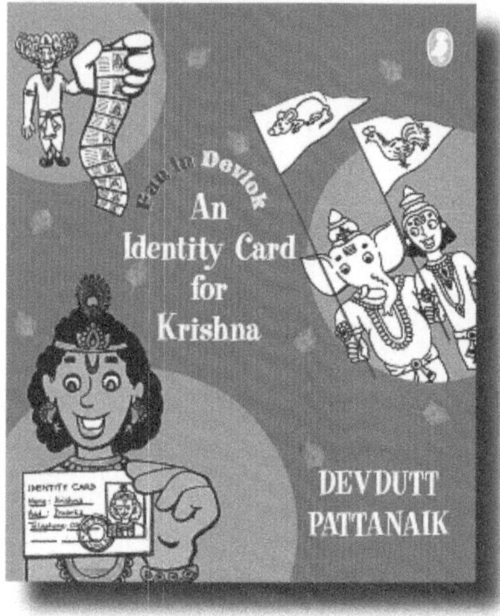

We all know that Krishna loved butter. Have you heard stories of Krishna stealing butter, and getting caught with an almost empty pot and a butter beard dangling from his chin? Well, there's something else Krishna loved: *avalakki*. *Avalakki* is the Kannada word for parched or flattened rice, also known as *poha* (in Hindi). There's a story of Sudama, Krishna's best friend, visiting Him and offering Him a handful of *avalakki* tied in a cloth as a present, since Sudama was very poor and couldn't afford to bring anything else. Krishna took the *avalakki* and ate it all up, hugged Sudama and thanked him. When Sudama returned to his humble hut in the village, he couldn't even recognize it because Krishna had turned it into a mansion. From then on, Krishna made sure that Sudama would never be short of food again.

There are so many stories about Krishna, which we all enjoy so much. But did you know that Krishna loved stories, too? Well, read this book to find out more!

Wait! How about making a little snack with Krishna's favourite ingredient, and *then* sitting down to read? It's easy to make and super delicious too!

FUN FACT! 'Avalakki Pavalakki' is a rhyme in Kannada, which doesn't really mean anything, but sounds fun. It goes like this: 'Avalakki-pavalakki-kanchina-mina-mina-daam-doom dus-pus-koi-kotaar'. What are some of the funny rhymes you know, and do they have a mention of food in them?

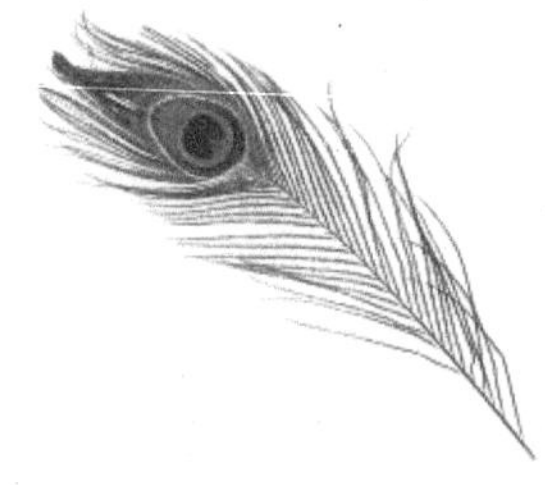

AVALAKKI PAVALAKKI

1 cup parched rice (*poha/avalakki*)

+

1 green cardamom

+

¼ cup grated or powdered organic jaggery, or to taste

2 tbsps warm milk, or as needed

+

2 tbsps grated fresh coconut

+

4–5 roasted cashew nuts

+

1 tbsp raisins

SERVES 2 PREP TIME: 30 MINS

KITCHEN GEAR: Sieve, pestle and mortar, bowl, spoon.

1. Put the parched rice in a sieve and wash it under running tap water for a few seconds. Drain well.

2. Set the sieve aside to let the rice soak for 10–15 minutes.

3. Meanwhile remove the seeds from the cardamom and grind them up to a powder in a pestle and mortar. (You can reserve the skin of the cardamom for mom's next cup of tea.)

4. In a medium bowl add the jaggery, milk, coconut and powdered cardamom seeds. Stir well.

5. Tip in the soaked parched rice.

6. Mix all the ingredients together with a spoon.

7. Top with the roasted cashew nuts and raisins. Eat right away!

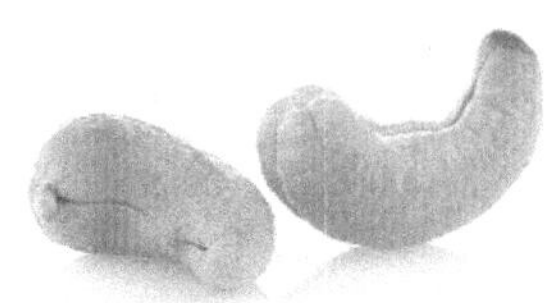

STREGA NONA
BY TOMIE DEPAOLA

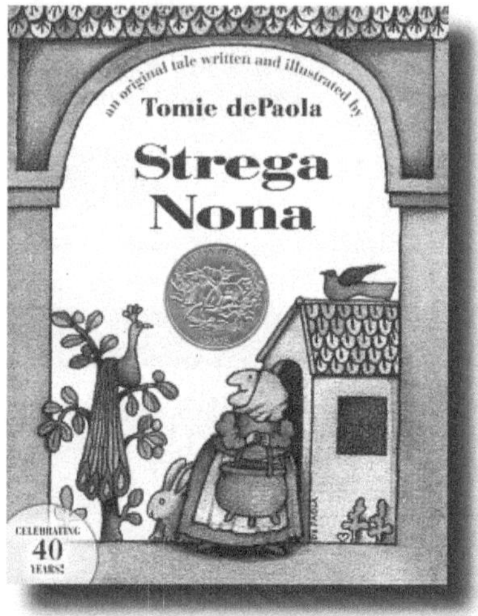

In this book, Strega Nona, or Grandma Witch, helps people with their troubles by using her magical powers. She also uses a secret spell on a pot to make lots and lots of pasta, and another secret spell to make it stop. Her assistant, Anthony, observes this from the sidelines, but doesn't pay careful attention at the end.

Do you wish you had a magic wand that would make things appear (or disappear) with just a wave and an the uttering of a magic mantra? How about getting a big bush of candied berries all to yourself with the first wave, and a bubbling chocolate fountain with the next one? Maybe you can get a gigantic plate of pumpkin pie if you so please, or a bottomless bowl of ice cream! Oh! That would be so much fun!

But what if, like Big Anthony in this book, you forget the magic mantra? And the candied berries, the chocolate fountain, the pumpkin pie and the ice cream, all continue to fluff and froth up until they fill your entire house? That would be quite a challenge, wouldn't it?

This Ma-corn-oni and Cheese, just like the pasta made by Strega Nona, will help you feel good, no matter what challenge you're facing. Ask a grown-up for help, and don't forget to say the magic word – please.

MA-CORN-ONI 'N' CHEESE

1 tbsp garlic and herb flavoured butter, soft

+

¼ cup cold milk

+

1 tsp cornflour

+

1 cup cooked macaroni or any short cut pasta, like shells or bowties

⅓ cup cooked corn kernels

+

Salt and pepper

+

25g cheddar cheese, grated

SERVES 1 ✶ PREP TIME: 15 MINS

KITCHEN GEAR: Medium microwave-safe (preferably glass) bowl, pair of oven mitts, fork, spoon, grater, plate, serving bowl.

1. Put the butter in a medium microwave-safe bowl.

2. Microwave for 30 seconds to melt the butter.

3. Meanwhile add the cornflour to the milk and stir well with a fork.

4. Pour the milk mixture into the melted butter. Stir well.

5. Microwave the mixture for 1 minute.

6. Add the macaroni and corn to the bowl.

7. Season lightly with salt and pepper. Stir.

8. Put the bowl back in the microwave and cook on high for 30 seconds.

9. Stir the cheese into the hot macaroni.

10. Ladle the pasta into a serving bowl and quickly eat it all up!

FUN FACT! Did you know that in the USA, July 14 is celebrated as 'National Mac and Cheese Day'? But Mac and Cheese tastes good on any day, doesn't it? Heehee!

LITTLE BEAR – BIRTHDAY SOUP
BY ELSE HOLMELUND MINARIK

How do you like to celebrate your birthday? Do you like bunches of balloons and streamers, tonnes of cookies and cream? Lots of games to play and prizes to be won? Peppy music playing out loud while you dance without skipping a beat? But more importantly, no matter how long it takes to bake, you can't have a birthday without a cake, can you?

Even if your mom forgets to time the oven when she's baking, she always knows when the cake is ready, just like she always knows when you're hungry, even if you're not right in front of her. If you want to help your mom in the kitchen, you can put on your chef's hat and cook something fun and easy, so she can work on other, more complicated things. That's exactly what Little Bear did, in this story, even though he was a little upset initially, when he assumed that his mom forgot his birthday cake! He stirred up some delicious and simple soup to enjoy with his friends on his birthday. And all is well that ends well, isn't it?

So, come on out with a ladle and a pot, and let's make some soup, good to dive into on any special day!

FUN FACT! While Little Bear put carrots, potatoes, peas and tomatoes in his birthday soup, in Korea, they make a soup with seaweed on birthdays! Do you want to learn how to pronounce the name of this Korean soup? Here, give it a try: It is called MiyeokGuk. That's Mee-yoh-kook.

*Chimichurri is an herb-based condiment from South America that is often served with grilled steaks.

VEGGIE SOUP WITH CHIMICHURRI

 +  +  +  + 

2 carrots | 1 medium potato | 1 large tomato | 12 pea pods | 1 tbsp olive oil

 +  + 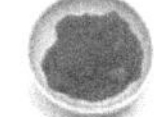 + 

Salt and pepper to taste | ½ tsp dried basil | 1 tbsp tomato paste | 2 cups vegetable stock

*For the Chimichurri**

 +  +  + 

¼ tsp lemon zest | 2 tbsps fresh parsley | 1 clove garlic | 1 tsp olive oil | Pinch of salt

SERVES 2–3 PREP TIME: 30 MINS

KITCHEN GEAR: Chopping board, peeler, knife, pressure cooker, wooden spatula, ladle, mortar and pestle, serving bowls.

1. Wash the vegetables and peel the carrot and potato.

2. Finely chop the carrots, potato and tomato.

3. Shell the peas into a small bowl. Set all these aside.

4. Pour the olive oil into a pressure cooker. Do not place it on the heat yet.

5. Add the chopped carrots, potato, tomato and the peas to the cooker.

6. Add the salt, pepper, dried basil, tomato paste and stock to the cooker.

7. Stir the soup 10 times.

8. Cover the pressure cooker with its lid and put on the weight.

9. Put the cooker on the stove on high heat. Reduce the heat when you hear the first whistle, and then let the soup cook for 5 minutes. Switch off the heat and allow the cooker to release steam on its own.

10. Meanwhile roughly pound all the ingredients for the Chimichurri in a mortar and pestle.

11. Ladle into the serving bowls and divide the Chimichurri topping between the bowls. Serve hot.

CURIOUS GEORGE
BY H.A. REY, MARGRET REY

Did you ever want to find out why the sky is blue, and why plants get dew? Why does the moon change its shape, and why do we yawn with our mouths agape? How does water turn to ice in the freezer, and a lemon juices up so well with a squeezer? Where does the sun go at night, and where do toads hide when it's light? Is the earth really round, and did a tiny bird just make that big sound? What happens if you mix red and green, and how do you go about meeting England's queen?

Too many questions to ask, too many things to find out. Where do you start, where does it all end? Our friend Curious George may have some of the answers, and give some clues to help you figure out the mysteries you always wanted to solve. Pick up any *Curious George* book and you'll learn how he discovers something fascinating, fun and new, each time.

And alongside, dig into this really delicious, Spunky Monkey Ice Cream, which we are sure Curious George himself would be quite pleased with!

SPUNKY MONKEY ICE CREAM

1 banana + 4–5 strawberries + 2 tbsps honey + A pinch of salt + 1 tsp multi-coloured sprinkles

SERVES 1 PREP TIME: 20 MINS FREEZING TIME: 2 HOURS

KITCHEN GEAR: Chopping board, knife, plate, food processor, silicone spatula, spoon, bowls.

1. Peel the banana and throw away the peel.

2. Cut the banana into slices and put it on a plate.

3. Wash and pat-dry the strawberries gently with an absorbent cloth/towel. Pull out and discard the strawberry leaves. Slice the berries and add them to the same plate.

4. Put the plate in the freezer and let the fruits freeze for about 2 hours, or until they become quite hard.

5. Put the frozen fruit into the jar of the food processor.

6. Add the honey and salt to the jar.

7. Run the food processor until the fruit turns into a smooth paste, stopping the machine a couple of times and scraping down the sides as needed. This will take a couple of minutes.

8. Use a spatula to scrape the ice cream out of the food processor and into a bowl. The ice cream will be soft and you can freeze it again for some time if you like a firmer texture.

9. Top the ice cream with the coloured sprinkles.

10. Well, what are you waiting for? Grab a spoon and dig in!

FUN FACT! Do you know that Curious George was known as Zozo in the UK when the book was first published there in 1941? That was done to avoid linking the name of a monkey with the king, as a mark of respect to King George VI.

RUNNY BABBIT
BY SHEL SILVERSTEIN

Want to have some fun with your fest briend? Wait, you didn't get that, yid dou? Trying to read that again, are you? Haha, yot gou! Er... got you!

In this fery vunny book called *Runny Babbit*, you will see a lot of uixed-mp words, oops... mixed-up words, and that is called 'spoonerism'. As you read along, you'll find that it is not only funny, but also a fun way to say things. For example, if someone's at the door, you might want to say out loud, 'I heard the roor-bell ding!' Or when you're going to sleep, you can take the book with you and announce, 'I love to bead in red!'

Runny Babbit fad a hamily, and they were all hery vappy, in their cozy hunny butch. Who's in four yamily, and who maughs the lost? When you've found the answers to these questions, don't forget to hump up jigh! And then you can enjoy a tall glass of this creamy, dreamy Marrot Cilkshake. Got it?

FUN FACT! 'Spoonerism' is named after Reverend William Archibald Spooner, an absent-minded Englishman, who often mixed up syllables in a phrase, not even realising that they sounded funny.

MARROT CILKSHAKE

 +  +  +  + 

1 carrot, chopped and steamed until soft	½ cup cold milk	1 small scoop butterscotch ice cream	A pinch of cinnamon powder	1–2 tsps organic jaggery/ organic jaggery powder or sugar to taste

SERVES 1 ✶ PREP TIME: 15 MINS

KITCHEN GEAR: Mixer-grinder, tall glass.

1. Add all the ingredients into the jar of the mixer-grinder.

2. Close the jar and turn on the mixer.

3. Count slowly to 10 and then turn off the mixer.

4. Pour the milkshake into a tall glass.

5. Bottoms up!

MASHA AND THE BEAR
A RUSSIAN FOLK TALE
TRANSLATED BY PETER TEMPEST

Do you know how to draw... a tree, a forest, a little girl, a hut, or a bear? Easy-peasy, lemon squeezy, did you say? Well, easy as pie for sure!

Take a plain paper, some colouring pencils or crayons, and get started right away. With the drawing, not the pie. Once you're done, open the book *Masha and the Bear*, and see how all those elements can make a wonderful story with a happy ending. Masha, a sweet little girl, wandered away from her friends while picking berries and lost her way. But if it wasn't for the friendly bear and the goodies he brought her from the forest, she would have been miserable, right? But since she still missed her grandparents, she plotted a clever little plan to re-unite with them and it worked like a charm! It wasn't all that easy, but Masha tried hard to make it a success.

So, just like Masha, why don't you get to work in the kitchen and help make a delicious pie? And hey, you don't have to hide under the pie! Just dig right in once it's ready to be eaten. And don't forget to share some with your Granny and Grandpa!

READER LEADER! If you liked *Masha and the Bear*, here's another Russian folktale you might enjoy: *The Tale of Tsarevich Ivan, the Firebird and the Grey Wolf.*

SAVOURY SNACK PIES

 +  +  +  + 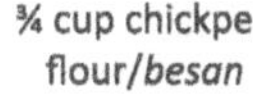

2 tbsps oil, divided

3 spring onions, green parts only, chopped

¾ cup chickpea flour/*besan*

½ tsp baking soda

½ tsp salt or to taste

 +  +  + 

Fresh ground pepper to taste

½ cup fresh tomato purée of 2–3 tomatoes

½ cup water

3 cherry tomatoes, optional

MAKES 6 PREP TIME: 15 MINS BAKING TIME: 40 MINS

KITCHEN GEAR: Oven, 6 silicone muffin cups, small baking tray, pastry brush, large sieve, mixing bowl, whisk, ladle, oven mitts.

1. Preheat the oven to 200°C/ 400°F.
2. Grease the bottom and sides of 6 muffin cups with a little of the oil using a pastry brush or your fingers. Place them on a small baking tray.
3. Sift the chickpea flour and baking soda into a mixing bowl.
4. Add the remaining oil, salt and pepper. Stir and set aside.
5. Strain the tomato purée and discard the seeds and skins.
6. Make a well in the centre of the flour mixture and pour in the tomato purée and water.
7. Whisk the mixture until smooth.
8. Add the spring onions and stir them in.
9. Divide the batter between the prepared cups.
10. Top each pie with one half of a cherry tomato (if using).

11. Place the tray in the oven.
12. Bake the pies for about 25 minutes or until they are light brown and set.
13. Remove the tray from the oven and let the pies cool for about 5 minutes before taking them out of their cases.
14. Dip your pie into a pool of tomato ketchup and wolf it down.

THE INCREDIBLE BOOK EATING BOY
BY OLIVER JEFFERS

We have all put funny things in our mouths when we were little. Some little ones like to chomp on things picked off the floor, while others go out to play and mouth a fistful of mud. Some others like to munch on chalk, while others like to chew on pencils. And then Henry, in this story, likes to eat books. The more he eats, the smarter he gets!

Imagine you had to survive only on strange things for a day. Imagine you had to eat vegetable skins and orange rind. Lemon seeds and banana peels. Peanut shells and corn-cobs.

Okay, okay, that would be weird. It could even make you sick! Relax, you're not actually going to eat any of that. Just some Choco Books. No, not the kind Henry ate in this story, but a real edible book made of chocolate. With a little help from a grown-up, you can make it and relish it, too, one small bite at a time.

FUN FACT! The author of this incredible book, Oliver Jeffers, is a bestselling author and artist who has won over 20 awards, three of which were for this book!

CHOCO BISCUIT BOOKS

 + 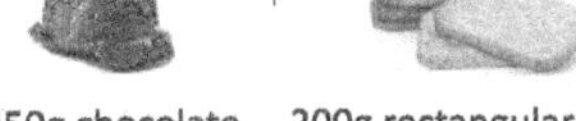 +  + 

250g chocolate ice cream

200g rectangular sweet biscuits (like Nice)

2 tbsps crushed walnuts

1 tsp chocolate sprinkles

SERVES 4 PREP TIME: 20 MINS FREEZING TIME: 2 HOURS

KITCHEN GEAR: Cling film, loaf tin or rectangular dish, spoon, serving platter, sharp knife.

1. Keep the ice cream on the counter so that it becomes soft.

2. Place a large piece of cling film inside the rectangular tin and fit it against the sides, with the excess overhanging on all sides. Set aside.

3. Put ¼ cup of the soft chocolate ice cream in the bottom of the prepared tin and spread it out evenly.

4. Now add a layer of the biscuits by making an even sheet of biscuits all over the ice cream, using smaller pieces if needed. Try not to leave any empty spots.

5. Repeat the ice cream and biscuit layers, for a total of 4-5 biscuit layers depending on the size of the tin.

6. Cover the tin with the overhanging cling film and put it in the freezer for a couple of hours or until firm.

7. Once the pudding has frozen solid, remove it from the freezer and open up the cling film.

8. Lift the pudding out of the tin using the cling film and put it upside down on the serving plate.

9. Peel off the cling film and discard it.

10. Cut the pudding into 4 'books' and top the covers with the walnuts and chocolate sprinkles. Serve right away. And if you need a bookmark to mark your page in the Chocolate Biscuit Books, you can always add a long, thin slice of apple or banana!

RAINBOW FISH
BY MARCUS PFISTER

The colours of the rainbow are fascinating in the sky, but they would be charming anywhere else too, like on the scales of a fish as described in this story.

But is it enough just to have colourful scales, if you're a fish? Or a nice dress or a shirt, if you're a human? No, you would have to be kind and polite, sharing and caring, and that's what matters. That's what will make you a good creature, small or big. Let's say your friend asks to borrow your new box of paints, or an exciting new toy you got, and you make a grumpy face and say, 'No!' Do you think that would make your friend, or you, feel good? The answer is no. If you share things with your friends, you will see that it will bring you closer, just like it did for the rainbow fish and his little fish friends in this story.

And to celebrate the story and the loving relationship between friends all over the world, we're making a cool and colourful snack! Do try it, and don't forget to share it with your family and friends, too!

FISH-SHAPED MEXICAN SNACK

 +  +  +  + 

½ cup boiled *rajma*

2 tbsps mild salsa

Salt and pepper

1 pre-made plain *khakhra* (Gujarati crisp roasted chapati)

1 cheese slice

 +  +  + 

5 roasted *makhana* (foxnuts)

1 cranberry or raisin

Half a cucumber, cut into half-moon slices

1 slice red radish

SERVES 1–2 PREP TIME: 20 MINS

KITCHEN GEAR: Shallow bowl, fork, spoon, serving plate, chopping board, butter knife.

1. Stir the salsa into the *rajma*. Taste and add salt and pepper if needed.

2. Place the *khakhra* on a serving plate and spread the rajma mixture all over it using a spoon.

3. Cut the cheese slice into a large triangle to make the head of the fish.

4. Make the fish's tail and fins by cutting the rest of the cheese slice into smaller triangles.

5. For the eye, use a *makhana* that has a bit of black skin on it.

6. Place a cranberry or raisin at the mouth of the fish.

7. Place the rest of the makhana near the fish's mouth as bubbles.

8. Use the cucumber slices to make the fish's fins.

9. Finish the rainbow fish with a slice of red radish in the middle of the fish's body.

FUN FACT! Use cut-out pieces of *bhindi* or lady's finger, dip them in acrylic paints and make a fish, bird or butterfly design on an old CD. Dab some glue once the paint is dry, and sprinkle glitter in different colours. Your very own version of a rainbow creature is ready!

PADMA GOES TO SPACE
BY SWETHA PRAKASH

Imagine you're flying high in outer space, just about to land on another planet or even the moon! All around you are fruity discs with shiny sprinkles, which you can pluck and gobble up for a quick snack if you're hungry. There is also a long flowing stream of comet juice that can be sipped on with a long straw from wherever you are.

You might discover similar fun things if you read this marvellous book: *Padma Goes to Space*. Padma, who goes to space, prefers Star Rock Salad to her mother's bhindi. Does the volcano ice cream she loves sound like something you'd love too? When you read the book, you'll find many more exciting things that you might like, and you'll have double the fun!

So how about a stellar snack? Try it, and you'll agree that it is truly out of this world!

TRY THIS! What's the one vegetable you would like to swap with an imaginary space food? Which planet would you like to visit, if you were to travel to outer space? Can you come up with names for stuff that grows in outer space? Make a scrapbook with your ideas and share it with your friends!

MILKY WAY GRAPE POPS

1 cup red grapes

+

1–2 cups 100% apple juice (based on the size of the pop moulds)

SERVES 4   PREP TIME: 15 MINS   FREEZING TIME: 4–6 HOURS

KITCHEN GEAR:
4 popsicle moulds*.

1. Put an equal number of the grapes into each of the popsicle moulds. You can cut the grapes in half if they are too big to fit in.

2. Fill the moulds with apple juice.

3. Put the popsicle sticks into the moulds.

4. Carefully put the moulds in the freezer and freeze for 4–6 hours, or overnight.

5. To unmould the pops, dip each mould in a container of warm water for a few seconds and then carefully pull the pop out using its stick.

6. Slurp on your popsicles on a super hot day.

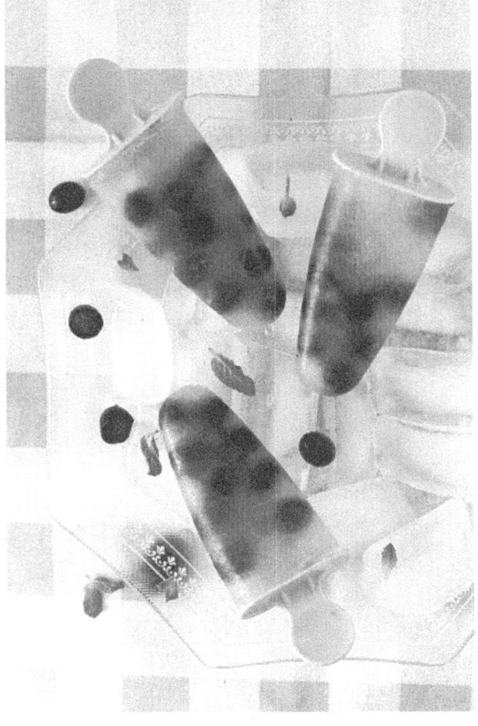

* You can also use small paper cups and wooden ice-cream sticks in place of the popsicle moulds. Put 4 paper cups on a small plate. Fill them as directed in the recipe. Now place a double sheet of aluminium foil over the cups and tuck it down the sides. Poke the wooden ice cream sticks through the foil into the centre of the cups. Place the plate in the freezer and freeze as directed. To unmould the pops, just tear away the foil and the paper cups.

RUMBLE IN THE JUNGLE
BY GILES ANDREAE

'Lions roar, eagles soar.
Buzzing bees, weevils on trees.
Hyenas howl, bears growl.
Swinging bats, scampering rats.'

The jungle is filled with so many kinds of creatures. Some eat during the day, while some at night find their prey, some sleep at night and others snooze off when it's broad daylight, some make sweet sounds and others just quietly do the rounds.

Do you have a favourite animal or bird? Is there one you're not too fond of, or are a little scared of? *Rumble in the Jungle* is a great book for you to learn all about them!

If there's a rumble in your tummy though, you had better fill it up with a healthy snack. Here's an easy recipe, if you like. Enjoy!

READER LEADER! The author and illustrator of this book, Giles Andreae and David Wojtowycz respectively, have created many more books that you might enjoy, like *Commotion in the Ocean*, *Dinosaurs Galore*, and *The Lion Who Wanted to Love*!

SLITHERING ORANGES WITH HONEY-YOGHURT DIP

1 orange

+

1 strawberry

+

2 chocolate chips

+

2 melon seeds

¼ cup yogurt, vanilla or plain

+

2 tsps honey

+

A pinch of cinnamon powder

+

1 tsp powdered cashews, optional

SERVES 1 ✶ PREP TIME: 10 MINS

KITCHEN GEAR: Serving plate, fork, dip bowl.

1. Peel the orange and remove and discard any extra pith.

2. Separate the orange into individual segments.

3. Arrange the orange segments to form the body of the snake.

4. Place the strawberry as the snake's head.

5. Push the chocolate chips into the strawberry for the snake's eyes.

6. Finally, poke the melon seeds into the strawberry to make the snake's forked tongue. Your Slithering Orange is ready.

7. Stir the yogurt with a fork until smooth. Add the honey, cinnamon powder and the powdered cashews (if using). Stir again.

8. Pour the yogurt into the dip bowl.

9. Serve your slithering snake with the yogurt dip on the side.

CATCH THAT CROCODILE
BY ANUSHKA RAVISHANKAR AND PULAK BISWAS

What would happen if you put a lion in a bird's nest? He won't quite fit in. Can you take a baby kangaroo and leave it on an alligator's snout? No, she might slide right into his mouth! And if you take a fish out of water, to leave it on a tree, it would be like taking the sun out of the sky and putting it on the earth. Everything has its place, and every creature has its separate home. Just like you and everyone else.

Catch That Crocodile is a funny story about a crocodile who got out of the water and started to tread on dry land. Read the story to find out if he was finally able to find his way back home.

Can you think of a vegetable or a fruit that looks like a crocodile? Here's a recipe for a *chatpata* snack that looks like a mean croc if you use your imagination. Make it, and sink your teeth right in!

FUN FACT! Crocodiles can live :
30 to 70 years. Some rare species
have lived for more than a 100 ye
them was 'Mr. Freshie', who is kn
lived to an estimated age of 120–
the Australia Zoo. He died in 201

CROCO-CORN ON THE COB

1 ear of corn + 3 tbsps mint leaves + 1 tbsp thick curd + ½ tsp chaat masala

SERVES 1 * PREP TIME: 20 MINS

KITCHEN GEAR: Serving plate, kitchen cloth, mixer-grinder, spoon.

1. Pull away the outer leaves of the corn so that the cob is exposed.

2. Roast the corn cob on the flames or boil it.

3. Wash and dry the mint leaves by patting gently between the folds of a clean cloth.

4. Put the mint, curd and the chaat masala in a small mixer jar.

5. Grind the mixture until smooth.

6. Put the cooked corn cob on a serving plate.

7. Spoon the green mint sauce all over your corn crocodile and it is ready for snack time!

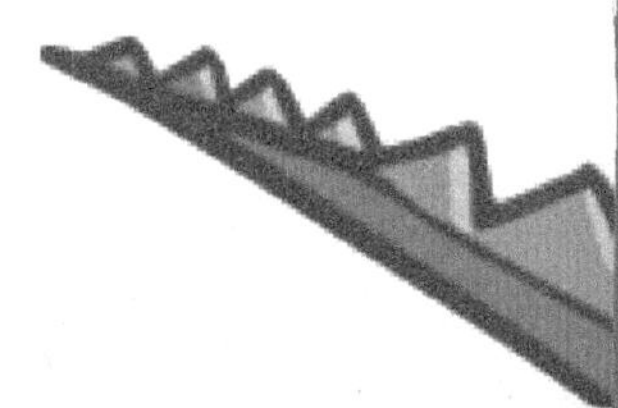

PEPPA PIG
BY NEVILLE ASTLEY, MARK BAKER, PHILLIP HALL

Peppa is a fine little pig, isn't she? You must have seen her jumping in muddy puddles, playing 'dress up', or hanging out with her little brother, George, and her soft toy, Teddy. There are many stories about and adventures of Peppa Pig, and they are all a lot of fun.

There is one about a Picnic, another about a Playgroup, one about Teddy's Day Out, and one more about a Traffic Jam. As you go through the Peppa Pig books, you'll see that Peppa loves food just like we all do. Some of her favourites are: pancakes and pizza, doughnuts and ice lollies, custard and pudding, tea and warm milk. How about we pick up a Peppa book and a peppy drink and go through them together? Here's a simple Pink Lemonade recipe that you can make with a little help from your parents, and you're all set for your Peppa Pig adventure!

TRY THIS! The Peppa Pig website has a cool 'Activity Maker'! You can choose an indoor or outdoor activity and the time you would like to spend doing it, too. Check it out!

PRETTY PINK LEMONADE

 +  +  +  + 

Quarter of a small beetroot | 5 tsps fine sugar or to taste | 500ml water | 1 lemon | A pinch of salt

SERVES 2 PREP TIME: 15 MINS

KITCHEN GEAR: Grater, muslin cloth, small bowl, jug, spoon, knife, lemon squeezer, 2 glasses.

1. Finely grate the beetroot and put it in a muslin cloth.

2. Squeeze the beetroot juice out into a small bowl. Set this aside and discard the beetroot shreds.

3. Put the sugar in a jug and pour in a little bit of the water.

4. Stir well with a spoon until the sugar gets dissolved.

5. Pour the beetroot juice into the mixture.

6. Cut the lemon in half.

7. Use a lemon squeezer to squeeze the lemon juice into the jug.

8. Add a pinch of salt to the jug.

9. Pour in the remaining water.

10. Stir well and then pour into serving glasses.

11. Add ice cubes if you like your drink cold.

12. Say 'Cheers!' and drink up.

THE MAGIC ROLLING PIN
BY VIKAS KHANNA

Do you believe in lucky charms? Maybe there's a little stone that you found when you were in a garden, and you always carry it with you in your pocket. Or a keepsake box filled with beads and baubles, feathers and flowers, leaves and laces, or things you found here and there. Things that you would never give to anyone and things that you never want to lose. More than all that, things that make you feel better and seem to bring you good luck.

In this book, *The Magic Rolling Pin,* Jugnu has his favourite rolling pin which he thinks helps him make perfectly round rotis. But when he has to go to the Gurudwara to make rotis, he loses his rolling pin. What happens then? Will Jugnu still be able to make round rotis? Find out by reading the book!

The author of this book, Vikas Khanna, is an award-winning chef who has many recipes and books to his credit. In fact, we think he will approve of a healthy snack made with wholewheat flour and jaggery, to help you keep up with the twists and turns in Jugnu's story.

With a little help, you can work your own magic on this recipe. As you'll see, all it takes is perseverance and patience!

TRY THIS! Can you think of more recipes that use a rolling pin? Puris, pies, pastries and tarts are some recipes that use it. Can you now think of other uses for a rolling pin? You can use it to crush pepper, for example, and to smash some garlic pods, too!

THE Magic ROLLING PIN

VIKAS KHANNA

ROLL-OUT ATTA COOKIES

 +  +  + 

1 tsp oil

1 cup wholewheat flour (atta)

½ tsp baking powder

1 tsp fennel powder

 +  +  + 

¼ tsp salt

60gm unsalted/ cooking butter, cold

⅓ cup powdered or grated organic jaggery with lumps removed

2–3 tbsps milk, or as required

MAKES 20 * PREP TIME: 30 MINS * BAKING TIME: 15 MINS

KITCHEN GEAR: Oven, baking tray, parchment/baking paper, scissors, pastry brush, sieve, mixing bowl, whisk, butter knife, cling film, oven mitts, cookie cutters, rolling pin.

1. Preheat your oven to 180°C/ 350°F.

2. Cut a sheet of parchment paper the size of the baking tray. Place it on the tray and set aside. Or use a large piece of aluminium foil to line the tray. Then, pour one teaspoon of oil on it and spread it all over, using a pastry brush or your fingers. Set aside.

3. Put the flour, baking powder, fennel powder and salt in a bowl and whisk well.

4. Meanwhile cut the butter into small pieces using a butter knife.

5. Add the butter pieces and the jaggery to the flour.

6. Use a fork or clean hands to mash the butter so that it gets crumbled up into the flour.

7. Add milk as required (one tablespoon at a time) and use your hands to pat the mixture together until a smooth dough forms.

8. Divide the dough in two parts and keep one aside, covered.

9. Roll out one part of the dough using your magic rolling pin to a thickness of about ¼ inches.

10. Dip a cookie cutter in a little flour and then press it into the dough to cut out a cookie. Repeat until you have cut the maximum possible cookies in the dough, dipping the cutter in the flour each time.

11. Use a butter knife to lift out the cookies and place them on the baking tray, about one inch apart from each other.

12. Repeat with the other half of the dough.

13. Wear oven mitts and put the tray in the oven. Bake for about 15 minutes or until the cookies start browning at the edges.

14. Allow the cookies to cool a few minutes on the baking tray before using tongs to place them on a cooling rack.

15. Let the cookies cool completely before storing them in a cookie jar. And don't forget to enjoy a few with a glass of juice!

THE ADVENTURES OF TOTO THE AUTO

BY RUTA VYAS

Have you travelled in an autorickshaw? There are cycle rickshaws and motor rickshaws, and, of course, both are fun to ride in. With the wind in your face and a swinging and swaying action as the auto pulls along, you get to see so many things up close, like shops and street-side sellers, people and animals, and all the colourful sights around.

In *The Adventures of Toto the Auto*, you will discover how Toto, the feisty autorickshaw and his driver Pattu go about solving problems, helping others and having loads of fun along the way. You will find out that it doesn't take a lot to be kind to someone, and that being brave is the best you can be.

Make sure you have this crunchy-munchy snack handy, before you ride along with Toto!

FUN FACT! Did you know that an auto is called by many other names, all over the world? Autorickshaw in India, trishaw in Sri Lanka and tuk-tuk in Thailand, maruwa in Nigeria, bajaj in Indonesia and baby taxi in Bangladesh.

MAKHANA MUNCHIES

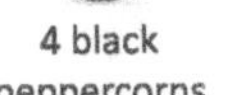

4 black peppercorns + 2 tsp ghee + 2 cups *makhana* (foxnuts) + ½ tsp black salt (*kala* namak) or chaat masala, to taste

SERVES 2 ✶ PREP TIME: 10 MINS

KITCHEN GEAR: Pestle and mortar, large microwave-safe bowl, oven mitts, ladle.

1. Grind the peppercorns to a coarse powder in a mortar and pestle. Set aside.

2. Put the ghee in a large microwave-safe bowl.

3. Microwave the ghee for 15 seconds or until it melts.

4. Bring the bowl out of the microwave and add the foxnuts. Toss well using a ladle.

5. Microwave the foxnuts for 1 minute on high power.

6. Wear oven mitts and remove the hot bowl from the microwave.

7. Toss the foxnuts using a ladle.

8. Return the bowl to the microwave and again cook for 1 minute on high power.

9. Wear oven mitts and remove the hot bowl from the microwave.

10. Add the black salt and ground pepper to the bowl. Toss well using a ladle.

11. Allow the foxnuts to cool down before eating or storing in an airtight container. The roasted nuts can be stored for about a week but we're sure they will be gobbled up long before that!

CLOUDY WITH A CHANCE OF MEATBALLS
BY JUDI BARRETT

We all know the power of imagination, and the effect it has on us when we read a story or watch a movie. In this wonderfully wacky book, you will see how people in the town of Chewandswallow face numerous kinds of challenges, all dictated by the weather.

Imagine, for a minute, that you live in this town. Big clouds of cotton candy falling like snow in the winter... Seems like a magical thing at first, but it would be boring and unhealthy, too, if that's all you got to eat all winter, wouldn't it? In the summer, perhaps you'd get to fill your pockets with crunchy salads made of rocket lettuce and other vegetables. How long do you think you could survive on this diet? Probably a day, or two, but definitely not all season long! So while all this sounds great in an imaginary world, we have to return to reality and cook our own food, no matter what the weather or season.

Still, if it is a recipe inspired by this wildly entertaining story, it can only make it that much more fun. Well, as long as the Masala Meatballs are snug in a pot and not raining down on us, right?

FOODIE FUN! Imagine a world where popcorn grew right out of the corn plants, or smoothies sprung out of fountains or streams! Gather your friends and write down a list of wacky, delicious foods that you could sample, straight out of the things around you. Compare notes and see who came up with the wackiest servings!

Cloudy With a Chance of Meatballs

Written by Judi Barrett and Drawn by Ron Barrett

Over three million copies sold!

MASALA MEATBALLS

½ cup soya granules/flakes

+

2 cups hot water

+

1 boiled potato

+

50g paneer

+

10–15 coriander leaves

1 slice wholewheat bread

+

¼ tsp salt

+

¼ tsp pepper

+

1 tsp tomato ketchup

+

1 tbsp oil plus more for greasing

+

¼ tsp garam masala

MAKES 12 PREP TIME: 30 MINS BAKING TIME: 20 MINS

KITCHEN GEAR: Oven, shallow baking dish or tray, pastry brush, sieve, 2 bowls, grater, knife, chopping board, plate, spoon, oven mitts.

1. Preheat the oven to 200°C/ 400°F.

2. Grease a baking dish generously with a teaspoon of oil and set aside.

3. Put the soya granules in a sieve and immerse the sieve in a larger bowl filled with the hot water. Set aside.

4. Peel the boiled potato and grate it into a large bowl. Grate the paneer into the same bowl.

5. Wash, dry and chop the coriander leaves. Add them to the bowl.

6. Lightly dampen the bread with water and then squeeze it out. Crumble up the soggy bread into the bowl.

7. Now add the salt, pepper, garam masala and ketchup. Set aside.

8. Squeeze the soya granules tightly to remove the excess water. Add the drained soya to the bowl and mix everything well.

9. Now take tablespoon-sized chunks of the mixture and roll them into meatballs. Place the meatballs on the greased baking dish and brush each one with oil.

10. Wear oven mitts and place the baking tray in the oven. Bake for 15–20 minutes or until lightly browned. Switch to grill mode for the last 5 minutes, to brown the tops.

11. Remove the tray from the oven and serve the meatballs with your choice of sauce.

NOTE! You could also shallow fry the meatballs in a nonstick pan with a little bit of oil, instead of baking them in the oven.

SECTION TWO

THE FAMOUS FIVE
BY ENID BLYTON

Enid Blyton may have packed great adventures into the Famous Five series, but there is more to these 21 books than just secret passageways, curious cases of missing objects, peculiar mysteries and sneaky smugglers. The Famous Five were a hungry pack, and they each had a favourite pick from the lavish spreads they were offered, whether it was indoors – with a proper table setting – or outdoors, on a comely picnic mat.

No matter which adventure you're a fan of, or which character you find most likeable, the descriptions of the food featured in the Famous Five books are definitely hunger-inducing. Good old teatime sandwiches and super salads with the crunch of fresh, dewy lettuce and the tang of tomatoes, steaming pots of porridge and too-big tureens filled with creamy mashed potatoes, light and airy ginger beer, dreamy, delicious macaroons and our top favourite – hot drop scones with runny butter.

Here's a current-day tribute to the scrumptious scones of the Famous Five series.

PSST!

If you absolutely love reading and eating together, these scones are your perfect bet! We say . . .

Eat them hot
And eat them a lot,
When caught in the middle of a Famous Five plot,
Seated in your favourite indoor or picnic spot!

SCOOP 'N' DROP CURRANT SCONES

 +  +  + 

⅓ cup unsalted/ cooking butter, cold

¾ cup dried currants or small raisins

1 tbsp cream or milk for topping

1–2 tsps sugar for topping

Dry Ingredients:

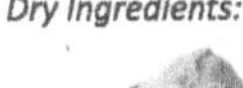
 + +  + 

1 cup wholewheat flour (atta)

1 cup all-purpose flour/*maida*

½ cup sugar, finely ground in a mixer

½ tsp salt

2 tsps baking powder

Wet Ingredients:

 +  + 

2 eggs

¼ cup curd

1 tsp vanilla extract

MAKES 12 PREP TIME: 25 MINS BAKING TIME: 25 MINS

KITCHEN GEAR: Oven, baking tray, parchment/baking paper or foil, butter knife, bowls – big and small, fork, pastry brush, oven mitts, tongs, cooling rack.

1. Preheat the oven to 180°C/ 350°F.
2. Line a baking tray with parchment paper, or use aluminium foil and grease well with oil. Set aside.
3. Cut the butter into small pieces and refrigerate.
4. In a large mixing bowl stir together the dry ingredients.
5. In another smaller bowl whisk all the wet ingredients.
6. Put the cold butter into the bowl with the dry ingredients and mash until mixed. Stir in the currants.
7. Pour in the wet ingredients and stir briefly with a fork to mix.
8. Now use two tablespoons to scoop and drop the dough in mounds onto the baking sheet, 2" apart.
9. Brush the scones with the cream and sprinkle with sugar.
10. Wear oven mitts and put the baking sheet in the oven. Bake for about 25 minutes or until the scones are golden and crusty.
11. Remove the tray from the oven. Cool the scones on a cooling rack before serving.

PETU PUMPKIN – TIFFIN THIEF

BY ARUNDHATI VENKATESH

Ever had the feeling, after a big fat meal, that you're still hungry? You're at a nice restaurant with your family, celebrating a birthday, and after munching your way through several platters of awesome appetizers, a massive main course, and drool-worthy dessert, you still have to have that extra piece of cake. Sounds familiar?

If you've read *Petu Pumpkin – Tiffin Thief*, or watched the movie, *Stanley ka Dabba*, you've probably felt a rumble in your tummy for something delicious. There's something about the description of food that always gets us, and it gets us right at that soft spot in our stomachs!

Imagine if you could just close your eyes and wander off into a fun fair – the smell of corn roasting on hot coal would drive you crazy. Perhaps you could also taste the sourness of the first batch of pickles at your grandmother's house in a moment's calling, and maybe the first rain of the season would remind you of the tang of raw mango, eaten with a sprinkling of salt and chilli powder.

Now all that has surely made you rather ravenous, and to help, we've put out an easy corn recipe for your immediate eating pleasure. If there's some left, you could take it in your tiffin box, too, like Petu. Just make sure no one else gets their hands on it before you do!

READER LEADER! If you enjoyed *Petu Pumpkin – Tiffin Thief*, do pick up *Petu Pumpkin – Tooth Troubles*, too!

CORN SUNDAL* WITH COCONUT CONFETTI

1 sprig curry leaves

½ lemon

+

2 tsps sesame, peanut or coconut oil

+

¼ tsp mustard seeds

+

Pinch of asafoetida

½ tsp split urad dal

+

1 tbsp roasted peanuts

+

1 cup cooked corn kernels

+

2 tbsps grated fresh coconut

+

2 pinches of salt

MAKES 2 SNACK TIFFINS ∗ PREP TIME: 20 MINS

KITCHEN GEAR: Chopping board, knife, lemon squeezer, small bowl, nonstick saucepan, spatula, spoon, tiffin box.

1. Wash and dry the curry leaves. Set aside.

2. Squeeze the lemon juice into a small bowl and discard the seeds. Set aside.

3. Put a small nonstick saucepan on medium heat and pour the oil into it.

4. When the oil is hot add the mustard seeds. Step away from the stove because the mustard seeds will now start to pop and might fly out of the pan.

5. When the sputtering has reduced, add the asafoetida, urad dal and roasted peanuts to the pan. Stir well.

6. Now add the corn kernels to the pan and stir. Cook for 1 minute.

7. Sprinkle in the grated fresh coconut and salt, and turn off the heat.

8. Pour the lemon juice into the *sundal** and mix well.

9. Let the *sundal* cool completely and then pack it in tiffin boxes.

FOODIE FACT:

**Sundal* is a dish from South India. It is usually made with varieties of cooked beans like chickpeas, black-eyed peas and whole moong dal.

THE JUNGLE BOOK
BY RUDYARD KIPLING

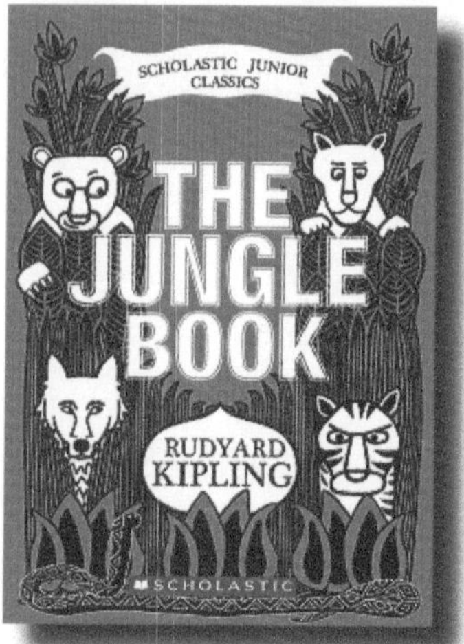

There are so many stories about jungles in books, right from the Panchatantra and Ramayana, and in movies like *Tarzan*, or *The Lion King*, that it's hard not to imagine being lost in one of them. Being lost in a jungle isn't necessarily a bad thing, as long as you know how to be safe, both from the physical threat posed by wild creatures and the unknown terrain, and the danger of poisonous plants and fruits. And of course, a sunny disposition would help a great deal, but even better if you could hum the *Lion King* theme song: Hakuna Matata – it means no worries!

Surely you've pictured yourself in a similar scenario, like Mowgli in *The Jungle Book*, cruising along a river that cuts through a mighty forest, or flying across tall firs and sequoias in deep, dark woods. If you had to survive for a little more than the span of this wild dream, in the thick of the jungle, you'd probably be better off reaching for fresh fruits.

A crisp, crunchy apple would keep the doctor away
And a fresh, juicy orange, the 'aachoos!' *at bay!*
A fistful of berries, or a dangling golden kiwi,
Would surely make you squeal, 'Whee, oh glee!'

Should you encounter a wild beast on your imaginary jungle trip, do think about Mowgli and how he fought the tiger, Shere Khan. Meanwhile, how does a pizza sound? Not just an ordinary pizza, but one approved for life in the wilderness, fictional or otherwise!

FUN FACT! Pench National Park in Madhya Pradesh, near Seoni, is the setting for *The Jungle Book* stories. However, did you know that Seoni, or Seeonee, is not an actual rainforest?

FRUITS OF THE JUNGLE PIZZA

1 tsp sugar

+

A pinch of cinnamon powder

+

1 pre-made plain paratha

+

2 tsps melted ghee

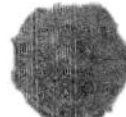
2 tbsps chocolate hazelnut spread like Nutella

+

5 strawberries

+

1 kiwi or chikoo

+

1 orange

SERVES 1 ✶ PREP TIME: 30 MINS

KITCHEN GEAR: Small bowl, pastry brush, *tava* or griddle, tongs, chopping board, knife, serving platter, spoon.

1. Mix the sugar and cinnamon in a small bowl and set aside.

2. Preheat a tava or griddle by setting it on medium-low heat for a minute.

3. Brush both sides of the paratha with the melted ghee, using the pastry brush.

4. Cook the paratha on the hot *tava* on both sides.

5. Remove the paratha on to a serving plate. Set aside.

6. Sprinkle half the cinnamon sugar mixture all over the hot paratha. Turn and sprinkle the rest on the other side. Cover and set aside.

7. Meanwhile wash and cut the strawberries into 2–3 slices each and set aside.

8. Peel the kiwi and cut it into slices. Set aside.

9. Peel the orange and remove the skin from the segments, if you want. Set aside.

10. Spread the chocolate hazelnut spread all over the paratha.

11. Arrange the fruit on top of the pizza, in a decorative pattern.

12. Cut into wedges and enjoy!

PIPPI LONGSTOCKING
BY ASTRID LINDGREN

We all have that one special friend who is a lot of fun to be around, and who cares for us when we most need it, and has our back all the time. Pippi Longstocking was that and more to Tommy and Annika!

If you want to be like Pippi, you could go on an adventure with your friends or even better, your BFF. Find-Keep, for instance, may be a great idea for one of those what-to-do weekend afternoons. You and your friend could go around the house looking for things to find, and, hopefully, keep – provided they're of no use to someone else, or willingly shared by them.

There are plenty of other kinds of adventures you could go on, like Pippi. Like jumping on one foot for as long as you can, going on a picnic in the backyard, or climbing up a tree for a tree-tea party on a solid branch. The possibilities are endless, and our Power-packed Pancakes will keep you going. Make sure you don't end up with egg yolk in your hair, if you happen to toss it up in the air to make it land in the bowl. (Oh well, even if you do, the yolk will only make your hair crackle and shine, like Pippi's!)

READER LEADER: Do you know Pippi's full name, as it is originally written in the Swedish book? It's a mouthful, and it is – Pippilotta Viktualia Rullgardina Krusmynta Efraimsdotter Långstrump! In English, it loosely translates as – Pippilotta Delicatessa Windowshade Mackrelmint Ephraim's Daughter Longstocking. Phew, that's quite a name!

POWER-PACKED PANCAKES

 +  +  + 

1 cup wholewheat flour	1 tbsp brown sugar	½ tsp cinnamon powder	½ tsp baking powder	¼ tsp baking soda	½ tsp salt

  +  +  +  + 

2 tbsps melted unsalted/cooking butter	1 egg*	1 cup thin curd	1 tsp vanilla extract	Ghee/oil for cooking the pancakes

MAKES 8 PREP TIME: 40 MINS COOKING TIME: 20 MINS

KITCHEN GEAR: Large and medium mixing bowls, whisk, nonstick *tava*, wooden spatula.

1. Put the flour, brown sugar, cinnamon, baking powder, baking soda and salt in a large mixing bowl.

2. Whisk these dry ingredients together. Set aside.

3. In another smaller bowl whisk the melted butter, egg, curd and vanilla.

4. Add the wet ingredients to the dry ingredients, and stir well.

5. Cover the bowl and let the batter rest for 10–15 minutes.

6. Preheat a nonstick *tava* on medium heat and drizzle with a little ghee/oil.

7. Pour about ¼ cup of the batter into the hot pan. Cook until the edges start drying and bubbles stop rising. Now flip and cook the other side. Remove the pancake to a serving plate.

8. Repeat step 7 with the remaining batter.

9. Eat the pancakes topped with a pat of butter and drizzles of honey.

* To make egg-free pancakes, stir together a tablespoon of flaxseed powder with ¼ cup warm water. Set this aside for 5 minutes and use it in place of the egg.

THE MAGIC DRUM & OTHER FAVOURITE STORIES

BY SUDHA MURTY

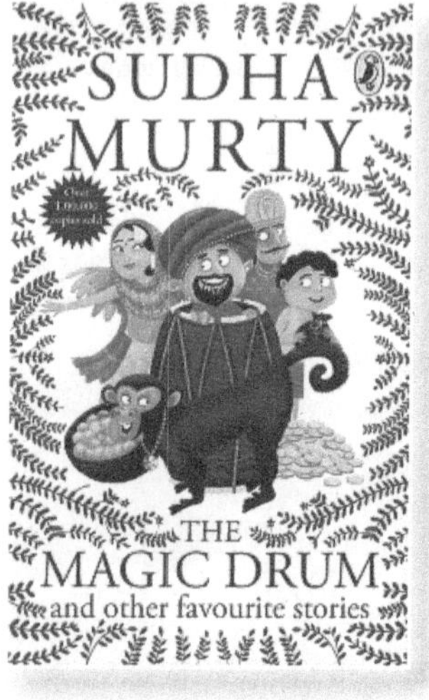

What's the one thing that both children and adults love? Chocolate? Could be. Pizza? Perhaps. Ice cream? Hmm. But the one other thing we all love is a good story.

Stories could come from anywhere, really: from the clouds up above or faraway lands, from next-door neighbours or great-granduncles. Stories have a beginning and an end, and they could start where something was lost or someone was found, and end in a place that was unknown, or in someone's favourite corner. They could be about anything, too: an amazing world adventure, or a funny little incident, a mystery that needs solving or the pursuit of a dear dream. Such is the magic of stories.

As you dig deep into these stories wonderfully retold by Sudha Murty, they will make you laugh, and feel for the characters in them. Whether you cheer for the old couple who got their lost bag of money back in 'The Magic Drum', or for the dog that got to lick the crumbs of 'The Last Laddoo'; whether you think about 'The White Crow', or the 'Horse in the Burrow', you will find this recipe for Mango Shrikhand Bars handy, to enjoy your way through the book.

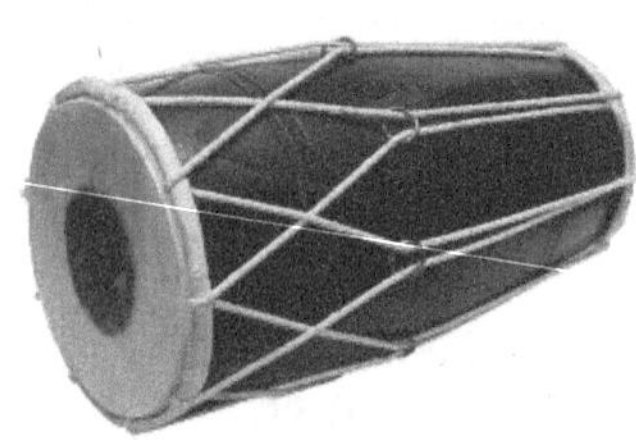

FROZEN MANGO SHRIKHAND BARS

 +  +  + 

1 cup mango *shrikhand*	2 tbsps chopped pistachios	2 tbsps white chocolate chips	½ cup fresh mango chunks

MAKES 12–15 ∗ PREP TIME: 10 MINS ∗ FREEZING TIME: 2 HOURS

KITCHEN GEAR: 8″ or 9″ tray that fits in your freezer, parchment/ baking paper or aluminium foil, ladle, spatula, knife.

1. Line a tray with a large piece of parchment paper or aluminium foil. Set aside.

2. Scrape the *shrikhand* into the middle of the prepared tray and then spread it into a rough rectangle using a spatula.

3. Scatter the pistachios, white chocolate chips and mango chunks on top of the *shrikhand*.

4. Place the tray in the freezer.

5. Freeze for at least 2 hours or overnight.

6. Take the tray out and quickly cut into squares using a knife.

7. Enjoy frozen.

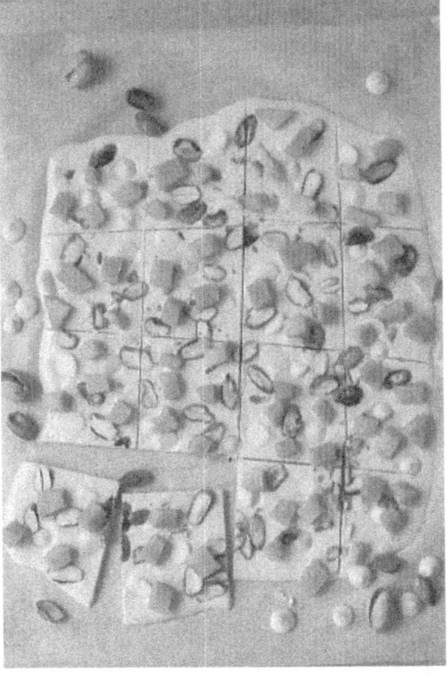

FUN FACT! *Shrikhand* is an ancient Indian dessert that is said to have existed as early as 400 BCE! It is very popular in Maharashtra, and is also relished in the state of Gujarat. It can be made with all kinds of flavours, like berries and figs, bananas and dates. You can also add rose essence to it – and this recipe, native to Gujarat, is popularly known as *shedki*.

HEIDI
BY JOHANNA SPYRI

As you know, life in the mountains is quite different from life in the city. The crisp air and the colour-kissed terrain, fresh root vegetables and tart berries, goat's milk and salt-cured meats, wildflower honey and the fragrance of green grass – these are just some of the things that people in the mountains thrive on.

When Heidi was taken to her gruff grandfather's house in the mountains by her aunt Dete, little did she know that she would come to love life there. It didn't take her long to make friends with the goatherd, Peter, along with whom, as you can read in this marvellous book, she went on many adventures around the cool vales and hills.

No matter where you are, the thought of a large chunk of cheese melting into a golden glob, like the sun, and tall glasses of slow-cooked, thickened milk swirled with delicious slabs of chocolate, leaving happy moustaches on the lips of drinkers, will make you smile. If this was the staple diet that kept Heidi happy and glowing up in the Alm, it wouldn't do bad for us either. Here's a twist to the customary creamy Hot Chocolate, mounted straight on a stick for your pleasure.

FUN FACT! Did you know that Heidiland (named after Heidi) is an important tourist area in Switzerland, and that 2521 Heidi is an asteroid, also named after Heidi? Isn't that cool?

HOT CHOCOLATE ON A STICK

+

150g dark chocolate (at least 40%)

1/4 of a 400g can of sweetened condensed milk

MAKES 8–12 PREP TIME: 15 MINS SETTING TIME 2 HOURS

KITCHEN GEAR: Large microwave-safe bowl, spoon, spatula, 8 silicone chocolate moulds or 8 silicone mini cupcake moulds or a silicone ice cube tray, wooden ice-cream sticks.

1. Roughly cut or break the chocolate into medium-sized pieces. Set aside.

2. Pour the condensed milk into a large microwave-safe bowl.

3. Microwave on high for a minute, ensuring that the milk does not overflow. If the milk boils up, stop the microwave, wait for 10 seconds and then restart it.

4. Wear oven mitts and remove the hot bowl from the microwave.

5. Add the chocolate to the bowl and stir until smooth, microwaving the bowl again on low power, if needed, to melt the chocolate completely.

6. Place the silicone moulds or ice-cube tray on a plate.

7. Carefully spoon the chocolate into the silicone moulds.

8. Push a wooden stick into the centre of each mould.

9. Let the fudge cool to room temperature, then refrigerate for about 2 hours.

10. Push the fudge sticks out from the bottom of the moulds.

11. To make a cup of hot chocolate, swirl a fudge stick or two in a cup of hot milk.

12. Store the fudge sticks in a box in the fridge.

ALICE IN WONDERLAND
BY LEWIS CARROLL

A rabbit hole would be a fun place to visit, smaller or bigger than our own worlds, depending on how we see ourselves fit in there. Not that we've ever been in one. Have you?! We've only 'been' in the rabbit hole that Alice went down, and enjoyed being there with her, through her many adventures and encounters.

The 'wonderland' that is described in this book has many spectacular things, enough to fascinate a child (or an adult). Some things are so strange that it makes us wonder what would happen if we tried to do similar things in real life. For instance, the drink that made Alice shrink, had a combination of weird flavours. Let's say we try to make something like that at home, by stirring up some tart berries and plum pudding, burnt toast and buttered clams in a big pitcher filled with ice and neem leaves. What would be the word to describe it – yum, or yuck? Haha, got you!

All through her visit to wonderland, Alice grows smaller and bigger until she finally comes back to her normal size, meets animals who are rude and polite, and sees the difference between what's imagined and what's real. While we can't re-create Alice's wonder world, we can balance the up and the down, the black and the white, and roll out a special recipe. These Psychedelic Pesto Pinwheels are not just awesome to look at, but also delicious to eat. They're fancy enough for a Merrymakers' Tea Party (whether or not you wear Mad Hats) with your friends, too!

READER LEADER! Author Lewis Carroll's real name was Charles Lutwidge Dodgson but he always wrote under the pseudonym, Lewis Carroll. You could try to be a bit like him: Put together a few sheets of paper and write about a dream in which you did things you probably couldn't do in real life. Draw a few pictures to go with the write-up, and your Dream Book is ready to share with your friends and family!

SCHOLASTIC JUNIOR CLASSICS

ALICE in WONDERLAND

LEWIS CARROLL

PSYCHEDELIC PESTO PINWHEELS

¼ cup hung curd, or cream cheese, at room temperature

+

1 tbsp pesto, any variety

+

1 tortilla or round plain parantha

+

¼ cup grated carrot

+

¼ cup thinly sliced purple cabbage

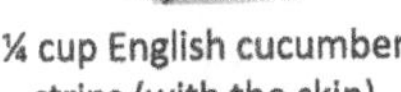

¼ cup English cucumber strips (with the skin)

+

¼ cup thinly sliced red capsicum

+

¼ cup pink radish strips (optional)

+

Salt and pepper

SERVES 1 PREP TIME: 15 MINS CHILLING TIME: 30 MINS

KITCHEN GEAR: Small bowl, whisk, chopping board, cling film, knife.

1. Put the hung curd/cream cheese in a small bowl and whisk until smooth.

2. Add the pesto to it. Whisk well.

3. Put the tortilla on a plate.

4. Spread the hung curd/cream cheese mixture all over the tortilla.

5. Place the carrot, cabbage, cucumber, red capsicum and pink radish (if using) over the tortilla in rows.

6. Sprinkle a little salt and pepper over the vegetables.

7. Now start at one end and roll up the tortilla tightly.

8. Cover the roll with cling film and put it in the fridge for half an hour or so.

9. Once the roll has chilled, remove the plastic film.

10. Place the roll on the chopping board and cut into ½-inch slices, using a knife with a sharp, serrated edge.

11. Arrange the pinwheels on a serving plate and they are ready to go.

CHARLIE AND THE CHOCOLATE FACTORY
BY ROALD DAHL

Chocolate can make some folks let out a ravenous roar and some of us go drip-drip-drool. It's easy to believe then, that the characters in this charming, chocolatey book were cuckoo-crazy about it.

Take Charlie, for instance, who got a Wonka chocolate bar every year for his birthday. Or Augustus Gloop, who could never have enough, and Veruca Salt, who always wanted more, more, more. The golden ticket was rather special then, to all of them, because it gave them a chance to go to Willy Wonka's chocolate factory and treat themselves to a splendid time.

Well, if you've read the book, you know what fate had in store for each of them. You also know that it turned out to be a golden day for Charlie, who not only loved chocolate, he got to make it and eat it too.

What are some of the chocolatey things that you like? Gooey brownies with a scoop of ice cream? Puffed-up bars of milk chocolate filled with dry fruits or wriggling rivers of caramel inside? A big glass of slightly spiced hot chocolate in winter? A delicious slice of chocolate cake? It's hard to pick one, isn't it? Or . . . how about some textured truffles made from crushed cookies? Well, we have just the right recipe for you – it's easy and fun to make, too. So, put on your chef's hat and get started right away!

FUN FACT! Did you know that there's a special Charlie and the Chocolate Factory attraction in the British theme park, Alton Towers? It's a fun ride where you get to go around the chocolate factory in little boats along a chocolate river, and much more!

WONKY COOKIE TRUFFLES

 +  +  +  + 

- 12 chocolate sandwich cookies like Oreo
- ⅓ cup smooth peanut butter
- ¼ cup icing sugar
- 1–2 tsp milk
- 1 tbsp multi-coloured sugar sprinkles

MAKES 8 PIECES PREP TIME: 30 MINS

KITCHEN GEAR: Food processor, two bowls, serving plate, butter paper, spoon.

1. Break up the cookies and put them in a food processor.

2. Run the processor until the cookies are ground to a fine powder.

3. Add the peanut butter to the processor and run until well mixed and almost like a dough. Add more peanut butter if required.

4. Transfer the dough to a bowl.

5. With clean hands, take tablespoon-sized pieces of the dough and shape them into truffles by pressing the dough in your fist.

6. Place the prepared truffles on a serving plate.

7. Sift the icing sugar on a piece of butter paper. Then lift the paper and siphon the sugar into a small bowl.

8. Add one teaspoon of milk to the sugar and stir until the glaze is smooth.

9. Use a small spoon to drizzle a quarter teaspoon of the glaze on each of the truffles and add a few sugar sprinkles.

10. Allow the glaze to set for 5 minutes before serving the truffles.

GERONIMO STILTON SERIES
CONCEIVED BY ELISABETTA DAMI

With more than 60 books in the series, and about 10 special editions, the Geronimo Stilton books are a big hit all over the world. They have been translated into 35 languages! How many of these books have you read? Which is your favourite one? Ours is *The Super Chef Contest*!

Well, no matter which one you pick, you've got to love all the books and all the Stiltons, for all their goofy adventures. The Rodent's Gazette may be the most 'famouse' newspaper in New Mouse City and it may carry several snippets of the latest goings-on in Geronimo's life, but to get a real glimpse into the Stilton family, you'd have to delve deep into the books.

Have you ever wanted to write for a newspaper? Or enter a cooking contest? We can help, on both counts, with a few tips and tricks from the mellow-mannered mouse, Geronimo. Never mind that he didn't know the first thing about cooking when he went on to become his cousin Trap's sous-chef. Maybe you can write about our book, and send it to your local newspaper. And maybe you can try this easy-as-pie recipe, too!

FUN FACT! There are at least four books in the Geronimo series that talk about different kinds of travel adventures. Do you know which they are?

Ans: *Down and Out Down Under*, *The Mystery in Venice*, *The Race Across America*, *The Discovery of America*!

DOUBLE CHEESE PIE

1 tbsp oil	2 tbsp breadcrumbs	½ cup wholewheat flour	¾ tsp baking powder	1 tbsp soft unsalted/ cooking butter	2 eggs

1 cup milk	½ tsp salt or to taste	Fresh ground pepper to taste	2 cups small broccoli florets	½ cup crumbled paneer	½ cup grated cheese – Cheddar or Gouda

SERVES 2 PREP TIME: 20 MINS BAKING TIME: 40 MINS

KITCHEN GEAR: Oven, pastry brush, 6" or 7" pie dish or baking dish, bowl, whisk, oven mitts.

1. Preheat the oven to 180°C/ 350°F.

2. Grease a 6" or 7" pie or baking dish with a tablespoon of oil using a pastry brush.

3. Sprinkle the breadcrumbs all over the base and sides of the dish. Set aside.

4. In large bowl, place the flour, baking powder and butter.

5. Use a fork to mix the butter into the flour.

6. Now add the eggs, milk, salt and pepper into the bowl.

7. Whisk well until the mixture is smooth. Set aside.

8. Put the broccoli in the prepared pie dish and spread it out.

9. Sprinkle the paneer and cheese evenly all over the broccoli.

10. Whisk the egg mixture once again and then pour it all over the broccoli.

11. Bake the pie for about 35-40 minutes or until puffy, lightly brown and set.

12. Remove from the oven and let the pie cool for about 10 minutes before slicing it into wedges.

MAGIC TREE HOUSE

BY MARY POPE OSBORNE

The Magic Tree House books are not just fun and entertaining; they also give you a sneak peek into several ancient events and places. Jack and Annie, the brother and sister team who are a part of these amazing historical adventures, are lucky to have the very magical tree house, right down the path from their home in Pennsylvania, USA.

Imagine, if you could be transported to a magical land – of yesteryear kings and queens, where wars were fought and monuments built. To a time when dinosaurs roamed the earth, or dragons were real, or say, to the North Pole, home of the polar bears, or the centre of a boiling hot, world-famous volcano. Perhaps to the abode of old writers, or to the home of the Pilgrim Fathers who went from Europe to America. Oh, the wonderful possibilities! But you know what the best part is? You can actually go to all these places – and no, you don't need a time-travel machine, or a magic watch, just these books!

If we were to pick one book that we love in this series, it would be a cakewalk to go with *Vacation under the Volcano*, for reasons that you'll soon see. Yes, we're making a Choco-volcano Cake, and that too, in a mug! However, if you want to know how it was to be in Rome on the eve of the eruption of Mt. Vesuvius, you'd have to read the book, with a scoop of the cake at the turn of every page, maybe!

FUN FACT! Did you know that when Mt. Vesuvius erupted, it released a huge cloud of stones, ash and fumes to a height of 33 kilometres? It is also the only volcano in Europe to have erupted within the last 100 years (it has erupted several times, actually), and is considered as one of the world's most dangerous volcanoes, too.

CHOCO-VOLCANO MUG CAKE

 +  +  +  + 

4 tbsp wholewheat flour (atta) | 3 tbsps powdered sugar | 1 tbsp cocoa powder | ¼ tsp baking soda | 1 tsp vinegar

 +  +  + 

1 tbsp vegetable oil | 3 tbsps milk | 2 squares of chocolate or a tbsp of chocolate chips | 2 large or 6 small marshmallows

SERVES 1 ✶ PREP TIME: 20 MINS

KITCHEN GEAR: Large microwave-safe mug, fork, oven mitts.

1. Add the flour, sugar, cocoa and baking soda to a large microwave-safe mug.

2. Stir with a fork until well mixed.

3. Pour in the vinegar, vegetable oil and milk.

4. Stir until smooth, using a fork.

5. Microwave the cake for 90 seconds on high power.

6. Wear oven mitts and remove the mug from the oven.

7. Break the chocolate into bits and place on top of the cake.

8. Also tear the marshmallows into pieces and place on top of the cake.

9. Microwave the cake again for 30 seconds or until the marshmallows melt.

10. The cake is best eaten immediately. It will be quite hot, so do be careful that you don't burn your tongue while eating!

THE TALE OF DESPEREAUX
BY KATE DiCAMILLO

In this award-winning book, we learn about Despereaux, the brave, big-eared mouse who rescued a princess (just like in the books he himself had read!) and the significance of soup, of all things. Yes, soup!

When Despereaux carried with him the aroma of an enchanting soup he had in the royal kitchen at Princess Pea's palace, several rats gathered and followed him around. Of course, you'd have to read the book from cover to cover, to uncover the mystery and mayhem in between.

If you've watched the movie, *The Tale of Despereaux*, which is loosely based on the book, you probably know all about the 'soup genie' that appears in the chief cook's pot. This genie, called Boldo, makes all his soups taste delicious.

So, speaking of soups, do you have a favourite kind? Soups can be hot or cold, spicy or sweet. They could be good for mending colds, and soothing for raging fevers. In honour of dear Despereaux and his French lineage (his mother, Antoinette, was French), we have here a magnificent mushroom-onion soup. Only, you'd have to actually stir and simmer it to a finish yourself – unless you can summon a genie for help with a blink of an eye!

READER LEADER! Kate DiCamillo, the author of this book, is one of only six authors in the world to win two Newbery Medals for her books – *The Tale of Despereaux* and *Flora and Ulysses*.

FRENCH-STYLE MUSHROOM SOUP

1 large onion

+

8–10 button mushrooms

+

1 tsp olive oil

+

1 tbsp unsalted/ cooking butter

+

1 bay leaf

+

½ tsp salt or to taste

¼ tsp black pepper powder

+

2 cups vegetable stock

+

7–8 fresh thyme stems or 1 tsp dried thyme

+

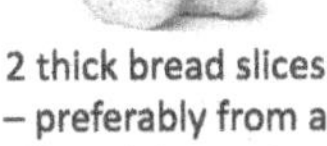
2 thick bread slices – preferably from a French baguette

+

2 tbsps grated Cheddar cheese

SERVES 2 PREP TIME: 1 HOUR

KITCHEN GEAR: Oven, chopping board, knife, soup pot, spatula, ladle, 2 shallow soup bowls, grater, baking tray, oven mitts.

1. Thinly slice the onion and mushrooms. Set aside.

2. Heat the olive oil and butter in a soup pot.

3. Add the onions and bay leaf. Cook on medium-low heat for about 15 minutes, stirring often, until the onions turn golden-brown.

4. Now stir in the sliced mushrooms and the thyme and cook for 5 minutes.

5. Add the salt, pepper and 2 cups of vegetable stock. Boil and then simmer the soup for 10 minutes.

6. Meanwhile preheat the grill of your oven.

7. Use tongs to remove and discard the bay leaf and thyme.

8. Transfer the soup to the serving bowls using a ladle.

9. Top each bowl with a thick slice of bread and sprinkle a tablespoon of cheese on it.

10. Place the bowls on a tray and place in the oven.

11. Grill for about 5 minutes or until the cheese is toasty and golden.

12. Wear oven mitts and remove the hot tray from the oven. Serve immediately.

THE LORAX
BY DR SEUSS

The Lorax, by Dr Seuss, is a very important book for all of us. This is because it talks about how humans, and their misdeeds on this planet called Earth, have done a lot of harm to Mother Nature. Chopping off trees, to name one such thing.

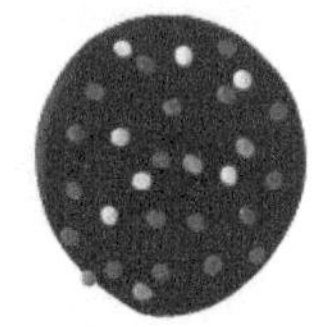

When you look around, do you see lovely green trees and hear the songs of birds the first thing in the morning? Do you smell fresh, garden-scented air when you're out? Unfortunately, not all of us do. We see few trees, and some lakes frothing up with dangerous chemicals. We hear the roar of engines and machines, and choke on puffs of black smoke.

Like the Once-ler, who lived in remorse at the far end of town after all the damage he had caused, told the boy in the story – that unless some of us really care, the destruction around us will remain a nightmare. It's time then to change the 'unless we care' to 'we will always care'. It's time, really, to speak up for the trees, like the Lorax did for the titanic Truffulas.

To celebrate the loving way in which Dr Seuss has taught us this important lesson, we're going to make these Chocolate Trees to enjoy. But let's also pledge to plant a real tree, when we can, shall we?

FUN FACT! Seuss Landing is a section in the Islands of Adventure theme park at Orlando, USA, based on the works of Dr Seuss. Some of the attractions are: Green Eggs and Ham Café, Hop on Pop Ice Cream Shop, and Moose Juice, Goose Juice!

CHOCOLATE TREES

\+

100g compound chocolate, your choice of dark or milk chocolate

Sugar sprinkles in different colours

MAKES 6 PREP TIME: 30 MINS

KITCHEN GEAR: A large tray that fits in your fridge, parchment/baking paper, scissors, small bowl – about 2" diameter, pencil, chopping board, knife, microwave-safe small bowl, spoon, 6 lollipop sticks.

1. Cut a piece of parchment paper the size of your tray.

2. Draw 6 circles of 2.5" diameter on the paper. Now turn the paper upside-down and place it on the tray. Set this aside.

3. Cut or break the chocolate into medium pieces and place in a microwave-safe bowl.

4. Microwave for 1 minute on low power and stir.

5. If the chocolate is not completely melted, microwave again on low power for 15–30 seconds. Stir until smooth.

6. Pour a tablespoon of melted chocolate into each of the 6 circles on the paper. Spread it evenly inside the outline using the back of the spoon. You can also transfer the chocolate into a squeeze bottle and then pour it out on to the circles.

7. Place a lollipop stick in each circle, such that about an inch of the stick is dipped inside the chocolate. Rotate the sticks so that the part inside the lollipop is covered in chocolate.

8. Use clean hands to drop the coloured sprinkles over each lollipop.

9. Put the tray in the fridge for 5 minutes to set the chocolate firmly.

10. The Chocolate Trees can now be lifted off the tray and straight into your mouth!

MR MAJEIKA AND THE DINNER LADY

BY HUMPHREY CARPENTER

Imagine if you or your teachers could appear in school at the press of a button? Or if things in the classroom could magically vanish, regular food in the cafeteria could turn into a feast, or bottles in the chemistry lab started to pour themselves out, creating a mysterious bubble-and-foam confusion. What a school that would be!

Well, in the Mr Majeika books, similar things happen in St Barty's Primary School in England. Mr Majeika is a wizard who zooms in, on his flying carpet, to teach Grade 3. His magical powers are revealed and also put to test many a time, through the series of books.

In this book – *Mr Majeika and the Dinner Lady* – the dinner lady, Mrs Chipchase, goes around making mealtime at school rather unpleasant for everyone in St Barty's, except her friend, Hamish Bigmore. But when Mr Majeika takes over, eating becomes a fun activity for the children. Right from baked beans to chips, fish fingers to ice cream, he serves them all the nice things, and the children forget all about the bony sausages and greasy noodles they were forced to eat earlier.

Here's a recipe for Mexican-style Quesadillas that you will enjoy, whether you're in school or at home, the park or a friend's house!

FOODIE FACT! The word quesadilla literally translates to 'little cheesy thing'. While most quesadillas are savoury, you could try your hand at a tasty sweet variation using sliced bananas and chocolate. Yummy?

ROTI QUESADILLAS

 +  +  + 

1 tomato | ¼ cup coriander leaves | 2 rotis | 50g processed cheese

 +  + 

½ cup boiled beans (like *rajma* or *lobia*) | Salt and pepper | 1 tbsp oil for cooking

SERVES 2 PREP TIME: 30 MINS

KITCHEN GEAR: Chopping board, knife, grater, *tava* or frying pan, large spatula, tongs.

1. Chop the tomato and the coriander leaves. Set aside.
2. Grate the cheese in a plate and divide it into 4 equal portions.
3. Set a roti on a plate and sprinkle one portion of the cheese over half of the roti.
4. Spread half of the beans, tomato and coriander leaves all over the cheese.
5. Sprinkle a little salt and pepper on top.
6. Sprinkle another portion of cheese over the beans and tomato.
7. Fold over the roti and set this aside.
8. Repeat steps 3–7 with the other roti.
9. Set a *tava* or frying pan on medium heat.
10. Lift the rotis using a large spatula and carefully set them on the hot pan.
11. Drizzle a little oil to help toast the quesadillas. Cook on both sides.
12. Place the quesadillas on a clean and dry chopping board.
13. Cut each quesadilla into three wedges.
14. Serve hot with plenty of salsa to dunk the wedges in.

DIARY OF A WIMPY KID
BY JEFF KINNEY

Do you have a journal that you write in regularly? Do you scribble little secrets in your Dear Diary every so often? Diaries are good for keeping secrets, but they are also good for memories. Usually when a year comes to an end, you like to think of all the memorable things that have happened over the year. And it's so easy if you've already jotted them down in a diary. Sometimes, even revisiting embarrassing or sad moments makes you realize just how much you have grown and how much you have learned.

The *Diary of a Wimpy Kid* is the journal of Greg Heffley, who was just entering middle school. It is a funny, quirky and satirical collection of his entries that will make you laugh and even sympathize with him from time to time. Whether it is about his little brother, Manny, who was a spoiled brat and got away with anything, or his run-in with a bunch of crazy teens on Halloween, his attempts to avoid the dreaded Cheese Touch – an imaginary disease caught by anyone who touched the mouldy glob of cheese on the basketball court and how it played a big role in his friendship with Rowley, or his dad's nagging about too much video-game time that Greg seemed to enjoy, his life was adventurous and fun. You will love going on this roller-coaster ride with Greg through his diary, feeling sad for him when he's in trouble, and elated when he scores big for a good deed done.

What you'll also love is this Sloppy Joes recipe with a delicious and nice touch of cheese, and maybe a favourite crunch-munch snack on the side.

FUN FACT! There's an online game called *Poptropica*, where players go to different 'islands' and overcome difficulties on different levels. Poptropica created two islands based on the Wimpy Kid series, called Wimpy Wonderland and Wimpy Boardwalk. The author, Jeff Kinney, is the Creative Director of Poptropica.

SLOPPY JOES WITH A TOUCH OF CHEESE

 +  +  +  +  +  + 

1 onion | 1 green capsicum | 4 cloves garlic | ¼ cup crushed walnuts | 200g block of paneer or tofu | 3 tomatoes | ½ cup corn kernels

 +  +  +  +  + 

Salt to taste | ¼ tsp cumin powder | ¼ tsp pepper | ¼ tsp red chilli powder | ¼ tsp dried thyme | 1 tbsp tomato ketchup

 +  +  +  +  + 

1 tbsp oil | 1 tsp vinegar | 1 tsp brown sugar | 1 tsp mustard sauce | 4 burger buns, preferably wholewheat | 4 cheese slices

SERVES 4 PREP TIME: 45 MINS

KITCHEN GEAR: Chopping board, knife, grater, mixer-grinder, saucepan, spatula, ladle.

1. Chop the onion, capsicum and garlic. Set aside.
2. Grind the tomatoes to a smooth puree. Set aside.
3. Grate the paneer and set aside.
4. Place a saucepan on medium heat with the oil. Add the onion, capsicum and garlic. Cook on low heat for 5–6 minutes.
5. Mix in the salt, cumin powder, pepper, red chilli powder and thyme.
6. Now pour in the puréed tomatoes and simmer until the sauce thickens.
7. Stir in the ketchup, vinegar, brown sugar and mustard.
8. Add the paneer, walnuts and corn to the sauce and cook for a minute.
9. Take the sauce off the heat. Set aside.

10. Place the bottom parts of the buns on a plate. Divide the Sloppy Joe sauce between the 4 buns.
11. Cut a few holes of different sizes in each cheese slice and place the slice on top of each bun. Place the bun tops on the sides.
12. Serve with chips, fries or sliced cucumbers.

THE TARANAUTS SERIES
BY ROOPA PAI

When playing a video game or watching a movie with 3D glasses on, you might have experienced the thrill of going through mazes and winding alleys, coming out of dark tunnels and emerging from fire-swept buildings in one piece, and solving puzzles that you may never encounter in real life. Such are some of the adventures that the characters in the Taranauts series – Zvala, daughter of fire; Tufan, son of the wind; Zarpa, daughter of Super Serpent Shay Sha – embark upon. They are called on to solve the 32 riddles hidden on the eight planets of the universe of Mithya by the very evil Shaap Azur, in order to bring light to Mithya, which is plunged in darkness.

Not only are the adventures in this eight-part series gritty and thrilling all at once, they are entertaining enough to make you want to grab a bowl of popcorn to munch through as you read the books. You'll soon figure out though that while your idea of a fun snack could well be popcorn, the Mithyakins eat some rather strange things. There's a 'samchori' – a combination of samosa and kachori, 'creposa' – a cross between a crêpe and a dosa, aamberry – a tango of mango and berry, batata fries – something between *batata-vada* and potato fries!

This imaginative and colourful world where the Taranauts tread is fun, addictive and enchanting. To help you through these intense pages of mysteries, races, riddles and quests, and keep a cool head all along, here's a recipe for brown Chocolate Snow.

READER LEADER! Where do you think the author gets the names for places, things and characters in the Taranauts series? From combining Hindi (or another Indian language) and English words in places, and sometimes, from being inspired by Indian mythology! 'Tara', is star in Hindi and the 'nauts' comes from 'astronauts'. Kay Laas, where Emperor ShoonYa lives, is from Kailash, where Lord Shiva is known to reside.

taranauts

ROOPA PAI

CHOCOLATE SNOW

 +  +  + 

1½ tbsps cocoa powder	½ cup powdered sugar or to taste	Pinch of salt	2 cups cold milk

SERVES 4 PREP TIME: 15 MINS FREEZING TIME: 2 HOURS

KITCHEN GEAR: Sieve, large mixing bowl, whisk, flat-bottomed metal pan or cake pan, fork.

1. Sift the cocoa powder into a large mixing bowl.
2. Whisk the powdered sugar and salt into the cocoa.
3. Add about a quarter cup of the milk to the cocoa.
4. Whisk until the sugar and cocoa dissolve into the milk.
5. Pour in the remaining milk and whisk until smooth.
6. Transfer the chocolate milk to a flat-bottomed metal pan. (A cake pan works well here.)
7. Put the pan into the freezer and freeze for an hour.
8. Bring out the pan and scrape the surface of the milk into snow using a fork. Keep scraping until no frozen chunks remain. Return the pan to the freezer.
9. Repeat this process twice, in intervals of 30 minutes, or until the mixture is slushy and frozen like snow.
10. Serve the chocolate snow in dessert bowls garnished with curls of chocolate if desired.

SECTION THREE

ASTERIX

BY RENÉ GOSCINNY & ALBERT UDERZO

TRANSLATED INTO ENGLISH BY DEREK HOCKRIDGE & ANTHEA BELL

Comics have a unique storytelling style that is unparalleled and one that words alone cannot do justice to. While it's just as easy to slip into an imaginative, visually rich world where word-books are concerned, it's rather fascinating to actually see the characters and settings depicted in comic books, frame by frame, as the story unfolds.

The Asterix series is packed with action, adventure, fun and fantasy. All the characters have their own unique abilities and peculiarities. Asterix's wit and warrior spirit, and his signature winged helmet, are right at the top of that list. These are followed closely by Obelix's charm and his standard, bow-tied hair, his quirky sense of humour and enormous appetite. Dogmatix, Obelix's pet dog, comes in third – he is a nature lover who howls and bawls when a tree is troubled, and is just as lovable for his sensitivity as he is for his intellect.

Following them on their adventures, we can hop in and out of just about anywhere on the world map, right from Spain to Switzerland, Belgium to the Middle East, tasting the local cuisines and getting a flavour of the local languages, too. Given that cheese is such a prominent part of so many of their expeditions, we thought a Cheese Fondue would be a good way to celebrate them and the rich comic-book legacy they have given us.

. GOSCINNY Asterix A. UDERZO

Asterix IN SWITZERLAND

Written by René GOSCINNY

Illustrated by Albert UDERZO

FUN-TASTIC CHEESE FONDUE

Fondue dippers – your choice of steamed broccoli or cauliflower florets, a carrot cut into thick sticks, 5–6 slices capsicum, toasted bread cubes, rusk, breadsticks or lavash

+

50g cheddar cheese

+

50g mozzarella cheese

+

1 tsp cornflour

A pinch of pepper powder

+

¼ tsp paprika or Kashmiri chilli powder, optional

+

2 tbsps milk

+

1 small garlic clove

SERVES 2   PREP TIME: 20 MINS

KITCHEN GEAR: Serving plate, grater, chopping board, food storage bag, medium microwave-safe bowl, oven mitts, spoon.

1. Arrange the fondue dippers around the edge of a serving plate and set aside.

2. Grate the cheeses on the chopping board.

3. Put the grated cheese in a food storage bag along with the cornflour, pepper and paprika (if using).

4. Close the bag securely and then shake it well. Set aside.

5. Now warm the milk in a medium microwave-safe bowl.

6. Peel and then grate the garlic clove into the bowl.

7. Transfer the cheese from the bag to the bowl. Stir.

8. Put the bowl in the microwave and cook on 50% power for 30 seconds.

9. Wear your oven mitts and remove the hot bowl from the microwave.

10. Stir once again, and if the cheese hasn't melted yet, microwave again for 15 seconds.

11. Carefully take the hot fondue to the table. You can also transfer it to a special fondue pot that has a tea light below the pot to keep the dish warm.

12. Use forks to spear the vegetables or bread, dip into the fondue and pop into your mouth.

13. In case the cheese starts to solidify you can return it to the microwave for a few seconds to warm up.

FUN FACT! Fondue has been around as the Swiss national dish since 1930. Gruyère cheese is the most used cheese in fondue, as it pairs well with many accompaniments, and holds its own when heated, without losing its sweet and salty flavour.

MALGUDI DAYS
BY R.K. NARAYAN

Counted as one of R.K. Narayan's finest works, *Malgudi Days* is a marvellous collection of short stories, set in the fictional town of Malgudi.

All the stories in the book bring alive the scenic beauty of Malgudi, and because some of the elements and characters are common to many of them, it's easy to imagine the town and its inhabitants as being real.

For instance, the Sarayu River, on whose banks the town of Malgudi stands, is a flowing undercurrent in many stories, providing ground for meetings and fasting stints. The restaurant without a name, The Boardless, is a place not to be missed, especially considering it is a hub for men who gather to discuss current events in Malgudi. Then there's the cobra, making an appearance in 'Naga' and 'The Snake Song'. There are the trees – the massive margosa, planted and cared for by Velan, and the tamarind tree, providing shade to significant characters, and sturdy boughs and ripe fruits for gambolling monkeys – standing tall and firm on the path leading up to the Town Hall.

As an ode to all these motifs in *Malgudi Days*, we have these tasty Tamarind Pops that can be put together in a trice. They'd quite possibly have won the approval of Swami and his friends too!

TANGY TAMARIND POPS

 +  +  + 

2 tbsps fine brown sugar

¾ cup deseeded dates

1 tbsp tamarind paste

¼ cup grated or powdered organic jaggery

 +  + 

1 tsp roasted cumin powder

¾ tsp black salt (*kala* namak)

¼ tsp red chilli powder

MAKES 10–12 * PREP TIME: 20 MINS

KITCHEN GEAR: Small bowl, food processor, serving plate or flat food storage box, 6–8 toothpicks.

1. Put the brown sugar in a bowl and set aside.

2. Put all the remaining ingredients – dates, tamarind paste, jaggery, cumin powder, black salt and red chilli powder – in a food processor and process until they get mixed thoroughly and become a smooth paste.

3. Scrape the paste into a shallow bowl.

4. With clean, dry hands, take a small chunk of the tamarind mixture and roll it into a ball.

5. Now put the ball in the bowl with the brown sugar and roll it so that it gets covered with sugar on all sides.

6. Put the candy on a serving plate or a flat food storage box.

7. Repeat steps 4 to 6 with the remaining mixture.

8. Stick a toothpick into each candy ball.

9. The tamarind candy is now ready to eat. The candy will stay good for about a week when stored in an airtight box.

FOODIE FACT! Tamarind has several uses: in cooking, it is used to add a sour taste to the food; because of its medicinal properties, it is spread on the forehead to reduce fevers; and in cleaning, it is used to shine brass and copper utensils.

THE PERCY JACKSON SERIES
BY RICK RIORDAN

It wasn't an easy life for Perseus aka Percy Jackson, in the Percy Jackson and the Olympians series, was it? Living with ADHD and dyslexia while fighting so many battles in the world of the mortals, both figuratively and literally. Learning about his half-brother, discovering his own strengths that sometimes turned out to be weaknesses. Roughing it out with the monsters, following which he scored, and later gave up several magical items like the bullet-and-sword-proof lion-skin coat off the Nemean lion, and the head of the Medusa off the gorgon. The list of the trials and tests he had to face is virtually endless.

It isn't always that we can go through stories like those of Percy's without attaching our own emotions to them, falling and rising with the hero, waiting with bated breath for the next page to bring an exciting victory, clenching our fists or gritting our teeth at a knockdown with an antagonist, feeling a stab in the heart and hoping, against all odds, that the one friend, or companion, of our hero, will magically appear to help when most needed.

Seeing that Percy's brain was wired to take to ancient Greek like fish to water (rather than English), in both culture and language, we have an offering that would clearly befit his style. It's a Greek Salad, but it's on skewers (in keeping with Percy's on-the-move way of life) – and who knows, it might help you take on big challenges as you get, set, go, too.

READER LEADER! You can have a Percy Jackson themed party with your friends, and treat them to these delicious Salad Skewers, among other things. Once there's enough food and drink to go around, you can sit in a circle and create your own Greek demigods. Outline their names, mannerisms, looks and special gifts. Write down what they love, and what they hate. Compare notes and see whose demigod seems the most powerful!

GREEK SALAD SKEWERS

1 onion + 1 english cucumber + 1 small zucchini + 1 small yellow capsicum + 8 cherry tomatoes + 8 olives + 2–3 leaves lettuce + 50g feta cheese

For the Dressing:

1 tbsp extra virgin olive oil + 1 tbsp lemon juice + 1 tsp honey + Salt and pepper to taste + 1 tbsp fresh oregano leaves or finely chopped mint leaves

SERVES 4 ✶ PREP TIME: 30 MINS

KITCHEN GEAR: Bowl, chopping board, knife, small tray, 8 bamboo skewers, serving plate, small bottle with tight lid.

1. Cut the onion into large segments and separate into layers.

2. Soak 8 of the largest onion pieces in a bowl with cold water to reduce the sharpness.

3. Wash all the remaining vegetables and drain.

4. Cut the cucumber and zucchini into thick slices. Set aside.

5. Cut the capsicum into large squares about the same size as the cucumber slices. Keep aside.

6. Drain away the soaking water from the onions and dry them.

7. Drain the olives and set aside.

8. Tear the lettuce leaves into 8 large pieces.

9. Take a skewer and push one piece of each vegetable on it, in any order you like. Fold up the lettuce leaves so that they are the same size as the other vegetables and skewer them.

10. Set the prepared skewer on the serving plate. Make 8 more skewers with the remaining vegetables, keeping them in the same order as the first skewer.

11. Crumble the feta cheese and sprinkle it on the skewers.

12. To make the dressing – put the ingredients in a small glass jar with a tight-fitting lid. Close the lid and shake the bottle well.

13. Drizzle the dressing on the skewers just before serving.

THE BOOK THIEF
BY MARKUS ZUSAK

Books set in the time of wars, especially the Second World War, aren't about the happiest of times. They are a window to a time when life was rough, and fear lurked everywhere. But how they touch our hearts!

In the same vein, *The Book Thief* has given us a fairly deep insight into the misery of Liesel, who lived in war-torn Germany. The coming-of-age story of Liesel actually goes from heart-wrenching to heartening, as we see her move from being shattered over her brother's death, to finding her path to freedom through the power of the written word. Books are her solace and retreat, and we see how they feed her soul and help her rise above her sorrow.

While supplies were scarce and pea soup is often referred to as the staple food of Liesel and her foster family, we'd like to toast this made-over version of a cheesy-peas gratin, to the unforgettable grit and spirit of Liesel, the gutsy and unforgettable Book Thief.

READER LEADER! The author, Markus Zusak, rewrote this book about 200 times, and he still wasn't sure anyone would be interested in reading it. But it went on to become a bestseller, and has sold more than eight million copies around the world!

* Gouda and Emmental are popular yellow, medium-hard cow's milk cheeses that originated in northern Europe. Try to find these or any German cheese in your supermarket, and if you can't, then just grate up some cheddar or processed cheese for this recipe.

CHEESY-PEASY GRATIN

 +  +  +  + 

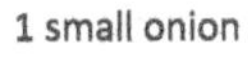

- 3 tbsps unsalted/ cooking butter, divided
- 1 small onion
- 1 large garlic clove
- 1 tsp dried parsley or thyme
- 2 tbsp wholewheat flour (*atta*)

 +  +  +  + 

- 1 cup hot milk
- 1 tsp mustard
- ½ cup grated Gouda or Emmental cheese*, divided
- ¼ cup breadcrumbs
- 2 cups cooked green peas

SERVES 2 PREP TIME: 30 MINS BAKING TIME: 15 MINS

KITCHEN GEAR: Oven, pastry brush, 6" baking dish, small saucepan, chopping board, knife, wooden spatula, whisk, small bowl, oven mitts, spoon, fork, grater.

1. Preheat the oven to 180°C/ 350°F.
2. Brush all sides of the baking dish with butter. Set aside.
3. Finely mince the onion and grate the garlic clove. Set aside.
4. Melt 1 tablespoon of butter in a saucepan and add the onion and garlic. Cook on low heat for about 2 minutes.
5. Stir in the dried parsley and the flour and cook until the flour darkens slightly.
6. Slowly pour the hot milk into the pan while whisking continuously. Cook until smooth and thickened.
7. Turn off the heat and stir in the mustard, ¼ cup of cheese and the peas.
8. Pour into the greased baking dish and sprinkle the remaining cheese. Set aside.
9. In a bowl microwave the remaining 1 tablespoon of butter and the breadcrumbs for 30 seconds, and stir.
10. Scatter the breadcrumb mixture over the peas gratin.
11. Wear oven mitts and place the gratin in the oven. Bake for about 15 minutes or until bubbling and golden.
12. Wear oven mitts and take the gratin out carefully. Serve hot!

THE CHRONICLES OF NARNIA
BY C.S. LEWIS

Narnia is everything that our world as we know it, is not, if you come to think of it. The ocean on the far east end has sweet water – good for thirst and hunger all the same; it is home to talking animals and mythological creatures; it is an integral part of a Multiverse (as opposed to our Universe); and it is a place where time stretches beyond the span of the clocks we are used to.

At the surface, this sounds fascinating in a one-dimensional sort of way. But as you go through the series, beginning with the revelation of the Narnia that was, to the time when it's all gone, you'll see, through the eyes of the Pevensies from our world and various Narnian inhabitants, that there are a lot more layers to every aspect of this magical, mystical world. There are horrors and there is magnificence, destruction and restoration, battles and moments of peace, doubt and clarity, despair and flashes of contentment that triumph brings, and there's an end, which is only just the beginning.

To this roller-coaster ride in a fantasy world that is Narnia, we pay a tribute with this warm and comforting Cinnamon-apple Bread Pudding. This dessert is royal enough to be eaten while seated firm on the highest throne in the house, like in Cair Paravel. And just like the apples on the trees planted by the Kings and Queens in Cair Paravel, this pudding is also as real as can be.

READER LEADER! The apple has been featured in books for a very long time, right from *Snow White and the Seven Dwarfs* (where Snow White was given a poisoned apple by the wicked queen) to Greek mythology (where Hercules had to bring a golden apple from Hera's orchard).

THE CHRONICLES OF
NARNIA
THE LION, THE WITCH AND THE WARDROBE
C.S.Lewis
BOOK 2

CINNAMON-APPLE BREAD PUDDING

 +  +  +  + 

3 tbsp unsalted/ cooking butter, soft

4 slices wholewheat bread

1 apple

2 tbsps raisins

2 tbsps chopped walnuts

For the Custard

 +  +  +  + 

¾ cup warm milk

2 eggs*

⅓ cup fine sugar

1 tsp cinnamon powder

1 tsp vanilla extract

SERVES 4 ∗ PREP TIME: 45 MINS ∗ BAKING TIME: 30 MINS

KITCHEN GEAR: Oven, pastry brush, 8" baking dish, chopping board, knife, peeler, large mixing bowl, whisk, wooden spatula, oven mitts.

1. Take a little butter and brush or rub it on the bottom and sides of the baking dish. Set aside.

2. Butter the bread on both sides using the remaining butter.

3. Trim away the crusts of the bread if you don't care for them. Cut the bread into cubes - 16 cubes per slice.

4. Spread the bread cubes in the prepared baking dish. Set aside.

5. Peel and then cut the apple into quarters. Remove the core. Chop the apple into small pieces.

6. Scatter the apple over the bread in the baking dish.

7. Also scatter the raisins and walnuts over the bread. Set aside.

8. Break the eggs into a large mixing bowl.

9. Add the sugar and whisk well.

10. Pour the milk in and whisk until smooth and the sugar dissolves.

11. Stir in the cinnamon powder and vanilla to complete the custard.

12. Pour the custard all over the bread in the baking dish. Push down all the bread with a spoon so that it soaks in the custard.

13. Cover the pudding and set aside for about 15 minutes.

14. Meanwhile, preheat the oven to 180°C/350°F.

15. Wear oven mitts and place the pudding in the oven. Bake for about 30 minutes or until the top is golden brown and the custard is set.

16. Wear the oven mitts again and carefully take the pudding out of the oven.

17. Serve hot with a jug of cream or scoops of vanilla ice cream.

* To make this pudding without eggs, use 1 cup of thin egg-free custard (made with custard powder) in place of the custard in this recipe. Pour this over the bread and apples, and bake as directed.

ROBINSON CRUSOE
BY DANIEL DEFOE

Sometimes it takes big, seemingly impossible strength to conquer challenges, for success to come our way. Like someone once said, 'When the going gets tough, the tough get going.'

The remarkable story of Robinson Crusoe is testimony to that. Being shipwrecked in a storm at sea, and then stranded on a deserted island for 28 years before finally being rescued, by pirates no less, was definitely no easy experience for Crusoe. He encountered cannibals and captives, fought against several odds, and built all his everyday essentials with his own hands, with the help of a few supplies and tools from the ship before it sank.

Crusoe had to find his way around a number of things, all of which we usually take for granted, for instance a calendar, or a clock, which come to our rescue when we need to keep track of our activities or appointments. Crusoe had to make do with markings on a wooden cross and handwritten records of his daily routine. He taught himself how to make candles and jars and bowls out of clay, grew rice and barley, made bread and wove baskets, grazed goats, and upon discovering an entire valley flush with grapes, learned how to use them well – he even dried them to make raisins.

In honour of Crusoe's struggles and successes, and the lessons they teach us, here's a recipe for Slushies done the tropical island way. You can almost taste the sunshine in every sip. Treat your friends and family to this drink and raise a toast to all the challenges you have overcome, together.

TROPICAL SUNRISE SLUSHIES

 +  +  + 

1 banana + 1 cup deseeded watermelon chunks + ¼ cup tender coconut water or water, as needed + 4 tsps honey or to taste

 + 

½ cup pineapple chunks + ¼ cup mango juice

SERVES 2 PREP TIME: 15 MINS FREEZING TIME: 2 HOURS

KITCHEN GEAR: Chopping board, knife, 2 bowls, mixer-grinder, 2 tall glasses, straws.

1. Peel and cut the banana into slices. Place in a bowl and put it in the freezer for a couple of hours or until frozen.

2. Put the watermelon chunks in a bowl and freeze them, too.

3. Once frozen, put the watermelon chunks and half the banana into a blender jar.

4. Add a little coconut water and two teaspoons of honey to the jar.

5. Blend until smooth, adding more coconut water as required so that it is thick but pourable in consistency.

6. Divide the watermelon slush equally between the two glasses.

7. Put the leftover banana, pineapple, mango juice and honey into the same jar.

8. Blend well until it is smooth.

9. Slowly pour the banana slush on top of the watermelon layer. Do not stir!

10. Add in straws and a paper umbrella if you like, and enjoy your slushies with a pal.

READER LEADER! Robinson Crusoe has been adapted into a pantomime, an opera, a serial, an animation series, a movie and comics. There's a Robinson Crusoe bookstore in Istanbul and a Crusoe Café in the UK!

MY FAMILY AND OTHER ANIMALS
BY GERALD DURRELL

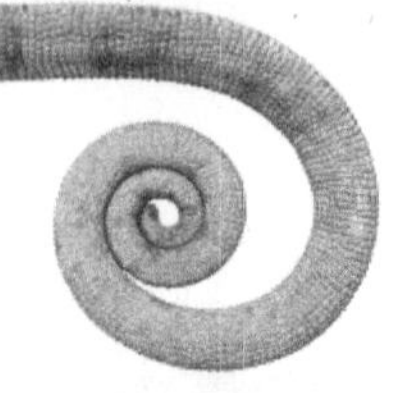

This is a funny, witty and engaging account of a part of naturalist Gerald Durrell's childhood that was spent on the island of Corfu, a Greek island. Even though it is called an autobiographical account, there are some fictionalized parts in the book. Gerry's love for animals is rather evident in the book, as is his interest in natural history.

Right from the Strawberry-pink Villa, the first house his family lived in when they set foot in Corfu, to the Snow-white Villa, the last one they called home before leaving for greener pastures, Gerry lugged along his many insect and animal friends with him, sometimes wreaking havoc and sometimes tickling everyone around him pink. Earwigs and beetles, geckos and goldfish, spiders and snakes, swallow-tail butterflies and flickering fireflies, turtles and toads, they all became a part of his colourful and entertaining life in Corfu as he went from his house to the garden, right up to the edge of the sea, to the marshy Chessboard Fields.

A perfect mishmash of light humour and serious nature-watching, this is one book that you simply cannot put down. What would go very well with it, then, is this recipe for a platter of chips-and-dip, done Greek style. You can't stop at just one serving, just like you can't stop at only one page of the book!

FOODIE FACT! Pita bread is a soft, yeasted flatbread believed to have originated in Mesopotamia, around 2500 BCE. It is popular all around the Mediterranean, and is very similar to the Indian flatbread, the naan. When cut in half, each piece has a pocket inside it that can be used to hold a meat or vegetable filling, making a boat-shaped sandwich.

CORFU HUMMUS WITH CRUNCHY CRUDITÉS

 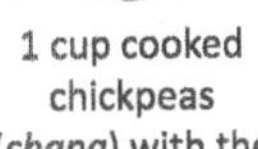     

3 cloves of garlic + 1 cup cooked chickpeas (*chana*) with the cooking liquid + 1 tbsp peanut butter + 1 tbsp lemon juice + 1 tbsp mint leaves + 2 tbsps extra virgin olive oil, divided

Salt and pepper to taste + A pinch of paprika or red chilli flakes + 1 English cucumber + 2 carrots + 2 wholewheat pita breads

SERVES 2 ✶ PREP TIME: 20 MINS

KITCHEN GEAR: Chopping board, knife, peeler, spoon, mixer-grinder, serving plate and bowl.

1. Peel and chop the garlic and put it in a mixer jar.

2. Add the chickpeas, peanut butter, lemon juice, mint leaves and 1 tablespoon olive oil.

3. Add 2 tablespoons of the reserved chickpea cooking liquid.

4. Add salt and pepper to taste.

5. Run the mixer-grinder until you get a thick, smooth, creamy paste.

6. Transfer the hummus to a serving bowl and use a spoon to swirl a circle into its surface.

7. Drizzle the remaining tablespoon of olive oil over the hummus.

8. Sprinkle the paprika over the top. Cover lightly and set aside.

9. Cut the cucumber and carrot into thick, short sticks.

10. Cut the pita breads into half, and then each half into 4 wedges.

11. Arrange the vegetables and pita around the hummus bowl and serve as a snack or appetizer.

ANNE OF GREEN GABLES
BY LUCY MAUD MONTGOMERY

Chronicling the life of Anne Shirley, a bright and chirpy 11-year-old orphan, who is sent from Nova Scotia to Green Gables by mistake, this book tells us so much more than just her story. It teaches us, above all, that friendship is a truly special gift and that choosing love over great opportunities that come our way, sometimes leads to greater things.

Often, the characters that we come to care for, be it in books or movies, stay with us for more reasons than one. It could be their appearance, demeanour, or how they deal with life situations. It could be their strengths, or their weaknesses, that we feel strongly about.

We are so often influenced by these moving characters that we use them as points of reference to deal with our own struggles and successes in life. From Anne, the one big lesson we learn is this: mishaps happen and we can't do a thing about that. For instance, trying to give ourselves a makeover by cutting off too much hair (or dyeing it the wrong colour, like Anne), could only cause that much damage. Well, if it's any comfort, it's only hair, it will grow back!

Wait, there's much more. Anne's love for books could be a great window of learning for us, too. Her dedication and determination, her confidence and caring nature – all tell us a thing or two about life.

To Anne Shirley, the sunshine girl who grew from strength to strength, we dedicate this Sugar-glazed Lemon Shortbread. Sounds like something her foster-mother Marilla would have baked, with her plum puffs for teatime, doesn't it? Come on, then, throw your friends an Avonlea tea party, with this sumptuous sweet treat!

READER LEADER! The Avonlea theme park in Canada allows tourists to dress up like characters in the Anne Shirley books and take pictures. There are also many souvenir shops around that sell girls' straw hats with sewn-in red braids and bottles of raspberry cordial soda – both based on descriptions in the books.

SUGAR-GLAZED LEMON SHORTBREAD

1 tsp oil
+

1 cup wholewheat flour (*atta*)
+
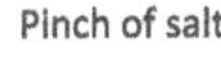
Pinch of salt
+

¼ tsp baking powder
+

⅓ plus ¼ cup icing sugar

100g unsalted/cooking butter, soft
+

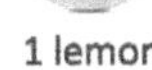
1 lemon

SERVES 4 PREP TIME: 20 MINS BAKING TIME: 30 MINS

KITCHEN GEAR: Oven, 7" or 8" round baking tin, parchment/ baking paper or foil, pencil, scissors, pastry brush, large sieve, butter paper, mixing bowl, electric beater, silicone spatula, zester or fine grater, small bowl, fork, spoon.

1. Preheat the oven to 180°C/350°F.
2. Cut a circle of parchment paper or foil the same size as the baking tin.
3. Grease the tin with oil. Place the circle inside. Brush oil over the circle. Set aside.
4. Sift together the flour, salt and baking powder. Set aside.
5. Separately sift the icing sugar.
6. Put the butter and ⅓ cup of the icing sugar in a large bowl.
7. Use an electric mixer to beat until the butter is light and fluffy.
8. Grate only the yellow part of the lemon skin (called the zest) into the bowl.
9. Add the flour mixture and mix well.
10. Spread the dough in the prepared pan and prick it all over with a fork.

11. Bake the shortbread for about 30 minutes or until the edges start to turn brown.
12. Wear oven mitts and remove the shortbread from the oven. Carefully cut into 8 wedges.
13. Put the remaining ¼ cup icing sugar in a bowl with a teaspoon of lemon juice and stir with a fork until it becomes a thick glaze, adding more juice if needed.
14. Drizzle the glaze over the completely cooled shortbread and let it set for 5 minutes.

THE MAGIC MOONLIGHT FLOWER AND ENCHANTING STORIES

BY SATYAJIT RAY

TRANSLATED BY ARUNAVA SINHA

Originally written in Bengali by master filmmaker Satyajit Ray, the stories in this book are a doorway to the beautiful landscape of our country. The stories stir a sense of curiosity in us, help us realize the merits of hope and honesty, all while we discover the simplicity and endearing little quirks of their characters.

Take, for example, the bird and animal lover, Sujan, in the first story. His only talent was that he could mimic a variety of birds and animals. But who knew that a little persistence and a spot of courage would take him to the palace, and eventually, to the Princess? A heart-warming story that brings us the mellifluous sounds of the birds and animals, and also teaches us to respect Nature and that every creature should be allowed the freedom to live in its own space.

In the story – *The Ogre and the Princess*, we are led to see the beauty in the Ogre, Ratan's voice, and in his heart. Ratan not only keeps the faith until the end, but also sees that his hope leads him to good things in his life.

There's so much to learn about life and love, about respect and goodwill, and above all, the importance of being honest and earnest, in these stories. To these beautiful thoughts and lessons, we toast our delicious Jhaal Muri. A simple, rustic snack from the Bengal region, it is great for evenings when the sun is going down and those pages are quickly turning.

SHARP 'N' SOUR JHAAL MURI

 +  +  +  +  + 

2 cups puffed rice	2 tbsps roasted peanuts	1 tbsp roasted chana dal	½ tsp black salt (*kala* namak)	½ tsp roasted cumin powder	¼ tsp red chilli powder

 +  +  +  +  + 

½ tsp chaat masala	1 boiled potato	1 small onion	2 Indian gooseberries (*amla*)	1 tbsp lemon juice or to taste	1 tbsp pre-smoked mustard oil

SERVES 2 PREP TIME: 15 MINS

KITCHEN GEAR: Mixing bowl, chopping board, knife, grater, ladle, paper cones or leaf bowls to serve.

1. Put the puffed rice, roasted peanuts and roasted chana dal in a large mixing bowl.
2. Add the spices – black salt, roasted cumin powder, red chilli powder and chaat masala to the bowl. Mix well. Set aside.
3. Peel and chop the boiled potato.
4. Peel and chop the onion.
5. Cut out the flesh from the gooseberry and discard the seed. Finely grate the flesh.
6. Add the potato, onion and gooseberry to the dry mixture in the bowl.
7. Drizzle the lemon juice and mustard oil all over the *jhaal muri.*
8. Take a large ladle and toss the mixture well.
9. Taste and add seasonings if required.
10. Serve the *jhaal muri* immediately in paper cones or leaf bowls.

FOODIE FACT! *Jhaal muri* is a very popular Indian street food that is unique to Kolkata, and it is known by different names (with a few variations in ingredients) in different parts of the country. In Karnataka, they call it *churmuri* and in Maharashtra, they call it *bhel puri.*

LIFE OF PI
BY YANN MARTEL

Life of Pi is a story of survival and spirit that outlines two main themes: that belief is everything in life, and that life is, quite simply, a story.

Pi or Piscine Patel's family, along with the animals from his father's zoo, was en route to Canada, aboard the *Tsimtsum*, a Japanese freighter, when they were hit by a storm. Pi survived, along with a handful of animals (a hyena, a zebra and an orangutan). Pi developed acute sensibilities and tactics when, after the animals were all gone – he was left alone with a tiger – whose name was Richard Parker. The story unfolds dramatically after this point, and in the end, you are left wondering about the line that separates truth and fiction.

Do you believe that life is a story, and that you can choose to tell it any way you want? Maybe if you talk to your parents, they'll tell you stories from their childhood, about silly fights, or the pranks they played with their friends or the secret plans they made. They'll probably stop and think for a while about the exact dates, times, places or names. If you want to save some special memories from your life, keeping a journal would probably help, or even a scrapbook, where you can stick pictures and write notes that you can revisit whenever you feel like it.

Here's a delicious cake to commemorate the beautiful story of Pi and the tiger, and the way in which their lives intertwined With alternating stripes of light and dark brown, it embodies not just the stripes on the tiger, but the ups and downs faced by the two of them, which they overcame with one strong weapon: belief. And that, we believe, simply takes the cake!

FUN FACT! Have you ever read a story written by an animal? Well, in the voice of an animal, by a human author. *Diary of a Killer Cat* by Anne Fine is the story of Tuffy, a straight-talking cat. It's a fun read and will keep you wondering whether Tuffy is the hero or the villain!

ROYAL BENGAL TIGER STRIPED CAKE

1 cup wholewheat flour (*atta*)

+

¾ cup grated or powdered organic jiggery, lumps removed

+

½ tsp baking soda

+

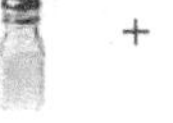

¼ tsp salt

+

¾ cup thin curd

1 tsp plus ¼ cup vegetable oil

+

½ tsp vanilla extract

+

1 tbsp cocoa powder

+

1 tbsp milk

SERVES 6 PREP TIME: 30 MINS BAKING TIME: 30 MINS

KITCHEN GEAR: Oven, 6" or 7" round baking tin, parchment/ baking paper or foil, pencil or pen, scissors, pastry brush, 2 mixing bowls, whisk, silicone spatula, 2 ladles, oven mitt, toothpick, cooling rack, cake plate or stand.

1. Preheat the oven to 180°C/ 350°F.

2. Cut a circle of parchment paper or foil the same size as the baking tin.

3. Grease the tin with oil. Place the circle inside. Brush oil over the circle. Set aside.

4. Whisk together the flour, jaggery, baking soda and salt in a mixing bowl. Set aside.

5. In a small bowl mix together the curd, oil and vanilla.

6. Pour the liquids into the mixing bowl with the flour mixture and whisk briefly.

7. Remove about half the batter into another bowl. Whisk in the cocoa powder and the milk. This is the chocolate batter.

8. Pour a ladleful of the plain batter into the centre of the pan and tap the pan lightly.

9. On top of the plain batter pour a ladle of chocolate batter.

10. Repeat with the remaining plain and chocolate batters, each time pouring the batter into the centre of the pan, on top of the previous layer. Tap the pan gently each time so that the batter settles.

11. Wear oven mitts and place the pan in the oven. Bake for about 30 minutes.

12. The cake is done when a toothpick inserted in its centre comes out without any wet batter or crumbs attached.

13. Allow the cake to cool for 5 minutes in the pan before running a knife carefully around the edges.

14. Now wear your oven mitts. Invert a cooling rack on top of the cake. Hold the rack and the cake together and turn upside down.

15. Remove the pan and discard the liner. Turn the cake right side up and cool completely.

LITTLE HOUSE ON THE PRAIRIE

BY LAURA INGALLS WILDER

Tall, wild grass covering the vast expanse of a prairie and the endless, boundless sky above it was all there was to the first view, when Laura's family got there by wagon after a long journey from Wisconsin and pitched a tent for their home. Laura's pa built a log house cabin for them to live in from scratch and their adventures started one after the other, with no end in sight.

Right from wolves surrounding their cabin to being robbed by hostile Indians, facing dire health threats and overcoming the severity of winters, the Ingalls family went through quite a series of troubles before they left the prairie in search of another home.

With a little help from neighbours who weren't exactly a stone's throw away, they relied on each other for small joys. Living through harsh conditions by supporting and comforting each other, they led an admirably decent life on the prairie.

The images that stay with us after we read this book, which is the third of nine in the Little House series, are definitely hard to shake off. And so is the food. Bread and cheese, cured meats and seasonal vegetables, raw honey and simple corn cakes. . .the delectable list could run into a couple of reams!

Simple rustic living was one of the highlights of Laura's life on the prairie. The cow's cream was rich and yellow in the summer, when the cows were fed 'good grass' that naturally made the butter durable and delicious. In the winter, they coloured the butter with carrot juice to fortify it and give it a warm glow. How about recreating that golden magic with some homemade butter? It is fairly simple, and you can add herbs to it for a wonderful, enriched flavour, too.

It would be great on hot toast or muffins . . . or just on its own, when no one's looking!

HOMEMADE HERB BUTTER

 +  +  +  +  

1 cup cream skimmed off the top of boiled and chilled milk (*malai*)	2 tbsps fresh mint leaves	¼ tsp salt	1 lemon	1 pod garlic

MAKES ¼ CUP ✶ PREP TIME: 30 MINS

KITCHEN GEAR: Mixing bowl, chopping board, knife, wooden churner or whisk, cup, butter dish.

1. Put the cream into a mixing bowl.

2. Whisk the cream well using a wooden churner or whisk, taking small breaks if you get tired.

3. As you whisk, the cream will first thicken and then separate into butter and liquid buttermilk.

4. Pour off the buttermilk into a cup, leaving the butter in the bowl.

5. Now pour a cup of ice and cold water into the bowl and set aside for 5 minutes. This will slightly harden the lumps of butter and wash it out.

6. Use clean hands to remove the lumps of butter. Squeeze the lumps well to remove any excess water. Put the butter in a bowl and set aside on the counter.

7. Meanwhile tear or chop the mint leaves using scissors or a knife.

8. Stir the mint and the salt into the butter using a spoon.

9. Grate the yellow part of the lemon skin (called the zest) into the butter and stir it in. Do not grate in the bitter white part of the skin.

10. Grate the garlic into the butter. Mix well.

11. Your herb butter can now be dolloped onto mashed potatoes, grilled corn...or whatever else you fancy!

FOODIE FACT! For a beautiful presentation, try moulding dollops of plain or herb butter in traditional butter moulds or small silicon chocolate or mini cupcake moulds. Push in the soft butter into the mould, smooth the top and let it set in the fridge until hard. Invert the butter out into a plate and scatter a few fresh edible flowers and herbs for a lovely display.

A SINGLE SHARD
BY LINDA SUE PARK

Set in the 12th century in Korea, *A Single Shard* is the story of a boy, Tree-ear, who lives with Crane-man, a physically handicapped straw-weaver, under a bridge in the village of Ch'ulp'o. They live on whatever they can find in the jungle and heaps of rubbish, on fallen grains of rice and other discarded edibles.

Tree-ear is fascinated by pottery and sneaks around the village, admiring the work of one of the finest craftsmen, Min. When he is caught in Min's backyard, dropping a box and breaking it into pieces, he is taken in to help for nine days as a way of repaying Min's debt. The nine days stretch into months and finally, he carries Min's work to show at the royal palace. Danger and disaster come calling and Tree-ear is able to only carry a shard of Min's work, which is so impressive in itself that the king commissions more work from Min.

Do you have a hobby, or a type of creative work that you absolutely love doing? Working on embroidery, painting and sketching, or knitting and weaving, can be an immersive experience. They all call for dedication, hard work and attention to detail. And Tree-ear not only learned all that, he also discovered his hidden creative talent, and he never lost hope.

To commemorate Tree-ear's positive and innovative spirit, here's a traditional Korean rice dish, joomukbap. It's easy and super fun to make and you can make a feast of it with your friends!

LINDA SUE PARK

A Single Shard

★"A timeless jewel." —*Kirkus Reviews*, starred review

JOOMUKBAP OR KOREAN FIST-RICE

1 tsp black sesame seeds

+

1 carrot

+

4 spring onions

+

2 cups cooked white or brown rice, lightly packed

+

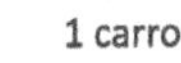

Salt to taste

1 tsp brown sugar

+

1 tsp soy sauce

+

¼ tsp red chilli sauce or to taste

+

1 heaped tbsp peanut butter

+

1 tsp sesame or peanut oil plus more for greasing

SERVES 2 ✶ PREP TIME: 40 MINS

KITCHEN GEAR: Microwave-safe mixing bowls – small and large, chopping board, knife, cup, fork, ladle, serving plate.

1. Put the sesame seeds in a small microwave-safe bowl and microwave for 30 seconds. Open the microwave, stir with a spoon. Then microwave again for 30 seconds. Set aside to cool.

2. Cut off and discard the top and bottom of the carrot. Peel and grate the carrot.

3. Trim away the spring onion roots. Chop the green and white parts into small pieces.

4. Set aside a few of the green spring onion pieces for garnishing later.

5. Put the carrot and spring onions in a large mixing bowl. Microwave this for 1 minute or until soft.

6. Add rice and salt to the mixing bowl with the vegetables.

7. Put the brown sugar, soy sauce, chilli sauce, peanut butter and oil in a cup and stir well with a fork. Microwave for 30 seconds.

8. Add the sauce mixture to the rice.

9. Add the toasted sesame seeds to the rice.

10. Mix everything together using a ladle or clean hands.

11. Now, grease your hands with a teaspoon of oil and make round balls with the rice mixture by pressing the mixture in your fist. Place the balls on the serving dish.

12. Wash your hands. Garnish the *joomukbap* with a tiny sliver of green spring onion and serve with sweet chilli dipping sauce.

FOODIE FACT! Rice balls like the Korean *joomukbap* are a common snack in many Asian cuisines, like the Japanese *onigiri* and the Chinese *zongzi*. Closer home, in Karnataka, leftover rice is flavoured with many condiments and mixed with curries, and traditionally fed to the younger ones by the parents as a 'fist ball' (*kai tuttu*, in the local language, Kannada).

WONDER
BY R.J. PALACIO

How often do we only 'look' at others before forming an opinion about them? Almost all the time. Some of the things we end up concluding in our heads are: he's so chubby, she's so tall, his legs are so long, her hair is so curly, his skin is so pimply, her nose looks crooked, his eyes are too small, her mouth is too wide, he must be so poor to look so shabby, she must be so rich to wear those expensive clothes.

When in fact, the things we 'look' at are hardly the keys to what those people really are like. Sometimes, looks are completely deceptive. What we look like doesn't actually tell you what we are like inside.

Wonder is a heartwarming story about August, a 10-year-old boy who had a rare facial deformity, which made him look different from everyone else. As if that wasn't enough to deal with, August gets bullied in school and faces challenges with friends. His struggles test him every step of the way, and he even loses his dog to cancer. But he never once stumbles – he keeps up a positive spirit and healthy attitude towards life, which in turn wins him accolades as well as the love and affection of his friends.

So while you enjoy this wonderful story of a remarkable boy, here's a warm and toasty cheese roll recipe that August himself would definitely approve of. He loved grilled cheese and warm chocolate milk, and maybe you can wash these Roll-ups down with a tall glass of frothy hot chocolate, too!

GRILLED CHEESE ROLL-UPS

4 slices wholegrain bread

+

4 cheese slices

+

½ tsp black peppercorns

+

½ tsp dried oregano

+

1–2 tbsps melted salted butter

SERVES 2 PREP TIME: 30 MINS

KITCHEN GEAR: Chopping board, knife, rolling pin, pastry brush, mortar and pestle, frying pan, tongs, serving plate.

1. Place the bread slices on a chopping board and trim away the crusts if you wish.

2. Flatten each slice by rolling it using a rolling pin a couple of times.

3. Brush the melted butter on one side of the slices.

4. Turn the slices so that the butter-brushed sides face down.

5. Unwrap and place one cheese slice on each bread slice.

6. Crack up the peppercorns coarsely in a mortar and pestle. Sprinkle the pepper and dried oregano over the cheese.

7. Now roll up each bread-and-cheese set tightly, and keep aside.

8. Brush a nonstick frying pan with the remaining butter.

9. Put the pan on the stove on medium heat.

10. Use tongs to place the rolls in the pan and let them cook until lightly browned.

11. Turn the rolls and cook on all the other sides, adding more butter to help them toast.

12. When the rolls are well-browned on all sides, place them on a serving plate. Eat them immediately - while they are hot and crispy.

FUN FACT! Cheese and bread are quite easily the most favoured food pair, dating back to ancient times. However, did you know that the grilled cheese sandwich is said to have originated in the 1920s, when sliced bread and American cheese both became readily available in the US?

A SERIES OF UNFORTUNATE EVENTS
BY LEMONY SNICKET

They say, out of great misery comes great hope. It couldn't have been better demonstrated than in *A Series of Unfortunate Events*, in which Lemony Snicket (the pen name of author Daniel Handler) serves as the narrator.

What didn't go wrong for the poor Baudelaire orphans? They lost their parents in a horrible accident, and were left with a monster of an uncle, Count Olaf, who wanted to get his hands on their princely inheritance one way or another. As they waded through several miseries during the course of the books in the series, there were a few moments of happiness, a few sparks that kept them going and smiling.

One of these moments came through in the first book – *The Bad Beginning* – when they were at the library of their kind neighbour, Justice Strauss, looking through cookbooks, as they had to prepare a dinner for Count Olaf and his guests. They happened upon a Pasta Puttanesca recipe, which they all agreed on, as it was easy and quick to make. It was all the more fun for them because Count Olaf detested it!

As the story unfolds further, you'll see how it's easy to dislike him, and that Pasta Puttanesca is indeed just what you'd want to dig into. So here's a fairly simple recipe for it. You could use 'interestingly shaped' noodles, like the Baudelaire siblings, or work with any pasta of your choice.

FOODIE FACT! In the movie *Lemony Snicket*, the children put this recipe together by finding some pasta in a dirty kitchen drawer, which they proceed to cook and strain through an old window screen. There are so many foods that can be similarly assembled by putting shreds and pieces of ingredients found scattered across your pantry or fridge – so go on, write your own food adventures!

PASTA PUTTANESCA

 +  +  +  +  + 

4 large tomatoes | 4 cloves garlic | 2 tbsps pitted sliced olives, any variety | 150g wholewheat spaghetti | 2 tbsps olive oil | 1 tbsp tomato paste

 +  +  +  + 

½ tsp chilli flakes | 2 tbsps capers, optional | Salt and pepper | ¼ cup fresh parsley | ¼ cup grated Parmesan cheese

SERVES 2 PREP TIME: 30 MINS

KITCHEN GEAR: Chopping board, grater, knife, large pot with lid, cup, frying pan, wooden spatula, colander.

1. Chop the tomatoes and set aside.

2. Peel and then grate the garlic. Set aside.

3. Chop up half the olives and set aside.

4. Cook the spaghetti as per the directions on the package. Save a cup of the pasta cooking liquid before draining.

5. Meanwhile set a large frying pan on medium heat with the olive oil.

6. Add the grated garlic and the chopped tomatoes and cook for 4-5 minutes.

7. Stir in the tomato paste, chilli flakes, chopped and sliced olives, and capers (if using). Season with salt and pepper.

8. Now stir in the cooked spaghetti along with a little of the reserved pasta cooking liquid if the sauce is too dry.

9. Finish the Pasta Puttanesca by garnishing with chopped fresh parsley and grated Parmesan cheese. Transfer to a serving dish and serve piping hot, along with a green salad.

ACKNOWLEDGEMENTS

First and foremost, we bow in deep gratitude till (our backs break or) the growls in our tummies begin to sound ominous, to our families. To our husbands, who patiently waited for the meals to be photographed or re-arranged before they could actually eat, and who made us several cups of tea that could occasionally have used a liberal wallop of sugar or heat (or both), to keep us going when we had our hands full with ovens dinging and skillets smoking.

To our darling daughters, who happily ate the crumbs and cuts of whatever we experimented with, sometimes too-salty, or less-sweet, super-spicy or underdone.

To our parents for cheering from the sidelines all through, even when it was clear we were up to no good, for buying us books and feeding us so many delicious meals and stories – it's hard to remember which was better.

To our friends who wholeheartedly support and endure us, who lend us their kitchen paraphernalia when we're short, and who always first ask, 'What's cooking?' even if they see that our hair is on fire. To be fair, they also sometimes send us the food they cook, the operative word being – sometimes.

To our agent, Kanishka Gupta, who picked us up when we had fallen, and emailed us late into the nights, demanding answers and making sure we weren't slacking off. And given our tendency to slip into food comas, that is quite a feat.

To our editor, Vatsala Kaul Banerjee, in whose unfailing enthusiasm we have found fuel for thought more often than not, and who always left a cheery note amid a pile of serious ones, helping us polish our efforts (not polish off) with dustings of sugar and cherries on top. She'll probably circle this and ask, 'Dried or fresh?' and we better have the answer ready.

To Nina Sud for being right on top of everything when we weren't, from the flow of words to the placement of pictorial props on the pages, and helping us get through several rounds of edits with her positive attitude and meticulousness. She deserves a long vacation in an undisclosed location, and we'll be sure not to disturb her with our silly anxieties and overenthusiasm.

To Roopa Pai, one of our favourite children's book authors, and in whose work for Hachette India – the Taranauts series – we have found inspiration not just for recipes (with quirky names to boot) but also for creative expression. We are thankful for her support and her effort in putting together such a heart-warming and encouraging foreword.

And last but certainly not the least – we are grateful for each other. We are so different and yet so alike, we have covered every shade in the rainbow with our moods and sensibilities, which go, at times, from the raging red of food snobs who don't accept invites to mediocre meals, to the light yellow of mellow fellows who can find satisfaction even in the cutting chai at the street corner. We have been through several ups and downs in life, fed each other everything from brick-like first breads to comforting *khichdi*s, and grown from strength to strength in our partnership – always bursting with new ideas and always egging each other on. We hope the spirit of our friendship remains ever intact and helps us rise above our follies and failures, as we continue to work together.

COPYRIGHT ACKNOWLEDGEMENTS

Page 8: Cover art for *Stone Soup* by Marcia Brown. Copyright © 1947 by Marcia Brown; copyright renewed © 1975 by Marcia Brown. Reprinted with the permission of Atheneum Books for Young Readers, an imprint of Simon & Schuster Children's Publishing Division. All rights reserved.

Page 18: Cover art for *An Identity Card for Krishna* by Devdutt Pattanaik reprinted with permission from Puffin India (an imprint of Penguin Random House).

Page 20: Cover art for *Strega Nona* by Tomie dePaola. Copyright © 1975 by Tomie dePaola. Reprinted with the permission of Simon & Schuster Books for Young Readers, an imprint of Simon & Schuster Children's Publishing Division. All rights reserved.

Page 24: Cover art for *Curious George* by H.A. Rey. Copyright © 1941, renewed 1969 by Margret E. Rey and H.A. Rey. Curious George, including without limitation the character's name and the character's likenesses, are registered trademarks of Houghton Mifflin Harcourt Publishing Company. Used by permission. All rights reserved.

Page 28: Cover art for *Masha and the Bear* reprinted with permission from B. Jain Publishers Pvt. Ltd.

Page 30: Cover art for *The Incredible Book Eating Boy* reprinted by permission of HarperCollins Publishers Ltd © 2016 Oliver Jeffers (book first published in 2006).

Page 34: Cover art for *Padma Goes to Space by* Swetha Prakash reprinted with permission from Tulika Publishers, Chennai, 2011

Page 43: Cover art for *The Magic Rolling Pin* by Vikas Khanna, illustrated by Mihir Joglekar, reprinted with permission from Puffin India (an imprint of Penguin Random House).

Page 46: Cover art for *Toto the Auto* by Ruta Vyas reprinted with permission from FunOKPlease Content Publishing Pvt Ltd.

Page 49: Cover art for *Cloudy with a Chance of Meatballs* by Judi Barrett, illustrated by Ron Barrett. Copyright © 1978 by Judi Barrett. Illustration copyright © 1978 by Ron Barrett. Reprinted with the permission of Atheneum Books for Young Readers, an imprint of Simon & Schuster Children's Publishing Division. All rights reserved.

Page 56: Cover art for *Petu Pumpkin – Tiffin Thief* by Arundhati Venkatesh reprinted with permission from Duckbill books

Page 58: Cover art for *The Jungle Book* by Rudyard Kipling reprinted with permission from Scholastic India Pvt. Ltd.

Page 62: Cover art for *The Magic Drum and Other Favourite Stories* by Sudha Murti, cover illustration by Priya Kuriyan, reprinted with permission from Puffin India (an imprint of Penguin Random House).

Page 64: Cover art for *Heidi* by Johanna Spyri reprinted with permission from Scholastic India Pvt. Ltd.

Page 67: Cover art for *Alice in Wonderland* by Lewis Carroll reprinted with permission from Scholastic India Pvt. Ltd.

Page 72: Cover art for Geronimo Stilton Series by Elisabetta Dami reprinted with permission from Scholastic India Pvt. Ltd.

Page 91: ASTERIX®- OBELIX®- IDEFIX® / © 2017 LES EDITIONS ALBERT RENE / GOSCINNY – UDERZO

Page 94: Cover art for *Malgudi Days* by R.K Narayan, illustrated by Lavanya Naidu, reprinted with permission from Puffin India (an imprint of Penguin Random House).

Page 101: Cover art for *Chronicles of Narnia* reprinted by permission of HarperCollins Publishers Ltd © 1950 C.S. Lewis.

ZBD
500
13/4/26

Cover art for *The Lion, the Witch and the Wardrobe* by C.S. Lewis copyright © C.S. Lewis pte. Ltd. 1950. Illustrations by Pauline Baynes © copyright CS Lewis Pte Ltd 1950. Reprinted by permission.

Page 104: Cover art for *Robinson Crusoe* by Daniel Defoe reprinted with permission of Scholastic India Pvt. Ltd.

Page 119: Cover art for *A Single Shard* by Linda Sue Park. Copyright © 2001 by Linda Sue Park. Used by permission of Houghton Mifflin Harcourt Publishing Company. All rights reserved.